RISE, RUIN & RESTORATION

A HISTORY OF SUTTER'S FORT

CHERYL ANNE STAPP

Cheryl Anne Stapp

Andrew Benzie Books
Walnut Creek, California

Published by Andrew Benzie Books
www.andrewbenziebooks.com

Printed in the United States of America

First Edition: April 2018

10 9 8 7 6 5 4 3 2 1

ISBN 978-1-941713-70-9

Library of Congress Catalog Number 2017918134

Cover and book design by Andrew Benzie

Dedicated to the memory of the California pioneers

TABLE OF CONTENTS

PART I

PART II

TIMELINE

1520 Hernán Cortés conquers Mexico for the Spanish Crown.

1542 Juan Cabrillo sails into San Diego Bay, which he names San Miguel, reaches Point Reyes where he is forced to turn back, and anchors in Monterey Bay. He dies on the Channel Islands and is buried there.

1579 Sir Francis Drake claims California for Queen Elizabeth I of England, naming it Nova Albion, but sails home without establishing a colony.

1603 Sebastián Vizcaíno rediscovers San Diego Bay and Monterey Bay, writes glowing reports of these ports, the fertile soils and agreeable climate—but finds no gold. Spain ignores California for another 167 years.

1769 Father Junipero Serra establishes the first of 21 California Missions, at San Diego. Traveling overland, Gaspar de Portolá, governor of Baja and Alta California, searches for Monterey Bay, but does not recognize it from Vizcaíno's description. His party includes the first Europeans to see San Francisco Bay, although they do not explore it, or name it. The steam engine is patented in England.

1770 Gaspar de Portolá successfully locates Monterey Bay, founds the Presidio of Monterey; declares it the capital of Alta California.

1774 The expedition led by Spaniard Juan Bautista de Anza opens a southern overland route to the California missions.

1775 American Revolution begins. Daniel Boone leads a party of settlers through the Allegheny Mountains to Kentucky.

1793 Scotsman Alexander Mackenzie, an employee of the Canadian-based North West Company, is the first white man to surmount the Rockies and reach the West Coast overland. He was looking for the mythical Northwest Passage. Eli Whitney invents the cotton gin, a machine that quickly and easily separates cotton fibers from their seeds, allowing for much greater production of cotton goods. The American textile industry is launched in Pawtucket, Maine, with the first cotton cloth manufacturing factory.

1797   New Jersey native Charles Newbold is issued the first U.S. patent for a cast-iron plow.

1803   The Louisiana Purchase adds 800,000 square miles to the United States, doubling its geographical size. Johan August Sutter is born in the Grand Duchy of Baden in southwest Germany.

1804   Lewis & Clark depart for a two-year expedition to explore and map the newly acquired Louisiana Territory, and on to the Pacific Ocean.

1812   The Russians establish Fort Ross near Bodega Bay. Robert Stuart and six companions engaged in the fur trade are the first white men to cross the Continental Divide through South Pass, traveling west to east. Although Stuart recognized it as the key to overland travel from the Atlantic to the Pacific coasts, the location was not widely known for another decade.

1814   Scottish seaman John Gilroy becomes the first foreigner to settle in Spanish California.

1818   Monterey is invaded and briefly "captured" by French-Argentine privateer Hipolito Bouchard.

1819   The canning industry is established in the United States. New Yorker Jethro Wood patents the iron plow with interchangeable parts.

1820   Advances in the manufacture of cast iron lead to the invention of the cook stove, women's first labor saving device. Small by later standards, this stove put the cooking surface at waist height for the first time, eliminating the need for precarious stooping and bending while lifting and moving heavy pots inside an open hearth. It was not available in California until 1849, when units were shipped around Cape Horn.

1821 Mexico wins independence from Spain, acquires California, whose residents learn of their change in national status in March 1822.

1825 Fort Vancouver established in Oregon Territory by the London-based Hudson's Bay Company (now merged with its rival, the North West Company), as headquarters for its western fur trade. The Erie Canal is completed, linking New York City with the Great Lakes.

1826 American frontiersman Jedediah Smith crosses from the Great Salt Lake region to California down the Virgin River and through the southern deserts.

1828 Jedediah Smith returns to California, traverses the Sacramento Valley and camps on the American River en route to Oregon.

1830 The first American-built locomotive makes its maiden run on the Baltimore & Ohio line.

1832 Captain Benjamin Bonneville and his caravan of 110 men and 20 wagons, traveling east to west, are the first group to take wagons across South Pass on the future Oregon-California Trail.

1833 Frontiersman Joseph R. Walker and his brigade of 40 fur trappers are the first white men to see Yosemite Valley.

1834 Mexico City orders the secularization of the California Missions; Swiss immigrant John Sutter lands at New York. Fort Laramie, Wyoming, and Fort Hall, Idaho (Oregon Territory), are built as trading posts for the fur trade. Cyrus McCormick patents his mechanical reaper; blacksmith John Lane devises the first steel plow, which he manufactured from old sawmill blades, in Lockport, Illinois.

1835 Taking a leave for his health, Harvard student Richard H. Dana Jr. signs on as a sailor on the trading vessel *Pilgrim*, and visits California ports. He publishes his experiences in 1840, entitled *Two Years Before the Mast*.

1836 Juan Alvarado becomes the first native-born governor of California. Texas revolutionaries are defeated at the Alamo. Fort Hall is sold to the Hudson's Bay Company.

1837   In Illinois, blacksmith John Deere invents the first commercially successful steel plow.

1838   John Sutter arrives at Fort Vancouver, overland from Missouri. Told it is too late in the season to continue south to California, he boards a ship for Hawaii.

1839   John Sutter arrives in the Sacramento Valley. The daguerreotype, the first photography process, is invented in France.

1840   There are fewer than 400 Americans and other foreigners living in Mexican California. Ninepins (early bowling) becomes a very popular game in America.

1841   Members of the four-year, world-wide scientific United States exploration party known as the Wilkes Expedition for its commanding officer, visit Sutter's Fort; the Bartleson-Bidwell Party arrives from Missouri. John Sutter buys Fort Ross. P. T. Barnum opens his American Museum in New York City, a combination zoo, wax museum, lecture hall, and freak show.

1843   The Joseph Chiles-Joseph Walker Party of about 40 people enter California at separate points; 1,000 individuals emigrate to Oregon in covered wagons. Jim Bridger and his partner establish Fort Bridger as a waystation for overlanders, in the southwest corner of Wyoming. In London, Charles Dickens publishes *A Christmas Carol.*

1844   Lt. John Charles Frémont and his Topographical Corps camp near Sutter's Fort for three weeks in March, to rest and replenish supplies. In November the Stephens-Murphy-Townsend Party brings the first wagons over the Sierra via Truckee (Donner) Pass. Samuel Morse sends his first telegraph message, from Washington, D.C. to Baltimore, Maryland.

1845   Captain John Sutter and his army of volunteers leave the Fort January 1 on an ill-fated campaign to fight Mexican rebels who want to overthrow Governor Manuel Micheltorena. James Marshall arrives at Sutter's Fort in July, from Oregon. John Charles Frémont arrives at Sutter's Fort December 10, on his second topographical expedition. Lansford Hastings publishes *The Emigrants' Guide to Oregon and California.*

1846   The United States declares war with Mexico, sends troops by
       land and sea to begin the conquest of California, and by
       agreement with Great Britain, acquires sole ownership of the
       Oregon Territory. The Bear Flag Revolt at Sonoma, in June, is
       eclipsed in July by the raising of the American Flag at Monte-
       rey by Commodore John Sloat, Commander of the Pacific
       Squadron. The massive Mormon migration from Illinois and
       other regions begins, and the largest numbers of overlanders
       to date arrive in California. Snow storms trap the Donner Par-
       ty at an alpine lake in the Sierra Nevada. Elias Howe patents
       his sewing machine in Massachusetts.

1847   In January, the Treaty of Cahuenga ends Mexican-American
       War hostilities on California soil. In March, survivors of the
       Donner Party are rescued and brought to Sutter's Fort. Mexi-
       co City falls to American troops in September. The Latter Day
       Saints establish a settlement in Utah. The first official postage
       stamp is issued by the U.S. government.

1848   James Marshall discovers gold in the tailrace of the mill he is
       building for John Sutter in the Coloma Valley. The Treaty of
       Guadalupe Hidalgo officially ends the Mexican-American War;
       California and vast southwestern lands are ceded to the United
       States. Captain William Warner, on leave from the Army
       Corps of Topographical Engineers, surveys and maps the
       city of Sacramento, assisted by Lt. William T. Sherman and
       Lt. Edward O.C. Ord. Several merchants rent space in
       Sutter's Fort.

1849   Thousands of American and European gold-seekers descend
       on California, with chaotic results. The *Alta California* (San
       Francisco) becomes the state's first daily newspaper. Sutter's
       Fort is sold to various individual buyers. California's first Con-
       stitutional Convention convenes in Monterey, declaring San
       Jose as the new capital. Pacific Mail Steamship Company be-
       gins service between San Francisco and Panama. Peter Burnett
       takes the oath as California's first elected governor. The safety
       pin is patented in New York.

1850   California is admitted to the Union as the 31st state. Fron-
       tiersman Jim Beckwourth discovers a Sierra Nevada moun-

tains pass; develops the Beckwourth Trail from Truckee Meadows, Nevada, to Marysville, California.

1852 Sacramento's Great Fire destroys 90 percent of the city; 761 new buildings rise within a month.

1854 Sacramento becomes the capital of California.

1856 The Sacramento Valley Railroad, the first railroad west of the Mississippi River, officially opens for business between Sacramento and Folsom.

1858 The Mason Jar is invented in Philadelphia, for use in home canning.

1860 The Pony Express commences cross-country mail delivery, simultaneously riding east from Sacramento and west from St. Joseph, Missouri.

1861 An attack on Fort Sumter opens the Civil War. Telegraph lines linking the American continent from coast to coast are completed; the Pony Express folds.

1863 The Central Pacific Railroad commences laying track eastward from Sacramento.

1865 General Lee surrenders at Appomattox, ending the Civil War. President Abraham Lincoln is assassinated in Washington, D.C.

1869 The Central Pacific and Union Pacific Railroads join at Promontory, Utah, to complete the nation's first continental railroad.

1874 Glidden barbed wire is patented.

1880 John Sutter dies in Washington, D.C. He is buried in Lititz, Pennsylvania, the town he resided in for many years.

1886 The History Company reissues several volumes of Hubert Howe Bancroft's seven-volume opus, *The History of California.*

1892 The first gasoline tractor with forward and reverse gears is built in Iowa by John Froelich, an American inventor.

1893 A restored Sutter's Fort is dedicated as a pioneer memorial.

PART I

INTRODUCTION

Brimming with hope and grandiose visions, Swiss immigrant John Augustus Sutter gave orders to land his little flotilla on the serpentine American River about two miles east from where it converged with the larger, wider Sacramento River. It was mid-August, 1839, and Sutter had already journeyed far and wide from his home in Burgdorf, Switzerland.

A string of failures marred his past, but energetic, ever-optimistic, thirty-six-year-old John Sutter was undaunted. Here in this place, here in this time, he was determined to erase his past disappointments and become the successful overlord of a self-sufficient trading post, and to establish a colony of Europeans from his homeland. Five years earlier he had fled Burgdorf in disgrace, narrowly escaping the looming reality of a Swiss debtors' prison for his bankrupt dry goods store. Landing in New York, he migrated to the Missouri frontier where he tried his luck as a Santa Fe trader, at first succeeding only to fail again in this and subsequent enterprises.

In April 1838, Sutter galloped away from Westport (now Kansas City) for a two thousand-mile trek with a fur caravan to Oregon Territory. He planned to travel overland from there into Mexican-owned California, where he had heard that fresh opportunities abounded. Arriving in Oregon too late in the season to ride south, he sailed to Hawaii, where he was marooned for five months. In July 1839 he at last landed at Monterey, after a detour to Sitka, Alaska.

John Sutter was not the first foreigner to establish residence in the northern climes of Mexican California. A Russian colony had been entrenched at their Fort Ross, near Bodega Bay, since 1812—though without official sanction from either Mexico or its predecessor, the Spanish Empire. Massachusetts-born Thomas Oliver Larkin had established himself as a respected Monterey merchant in 1833. Harvard graduate John Marsh had entered Los Angeles in 1836 via a southern route, and now lived some forty miles inland from the eastern shore of San Francisco Bay. Missourian George Yount had arrived at Mission San Gabriel in 1831. He received the nearly

12,000-acre Rancho Caymus, in the Napa Valley, as a Mexican land grant in 1836.

Sutter established friendly relations with the Russians, and purchased supplies from Thomas Larkin. He met and befriended his closest neighbors John Marsh and George Yount. Years later, much to Sutter's chagrin, Yount's presence lured scores of immigrants away from the Sacramento Valley to the lush landscapes surrounding the Rancho Caymus.

John A. Sutter in 1839. *Author's collection.*

There was a sprinkling of others: Englishmen, Scots, Americans, and at least one expatriate Spaniard, most of them living in coastal regions. John Sutter, though, was the only settler in the huge Sacramento Valley. There was no city or Euro-American settlement of any kind anywhere in the Valley before he arrived. The region was a wilderness inhabited by indigenous Indian tribes, but no white settlers of any nation.

Remaining with Sutter that August day after he dispatched the hired schooners *Isabel* and *Nicholas* back to San Francisco Bay, were two or three European craftsmen he had met during his travels, and ten Hawaiians he had hired in the Islands as laborers under a three-year contract. Walking south from the American River, he chose a site just beyond a meandering slough where the land rose in a knoll above the plains. The Hawaiians quickly fashioned huts from the nearby tule reeds. Sutter himself lived in a tent until his employees erected a forty-foot-long, one-story adobe building, thatched with tules that later burned. This structure was partitioned into three rooms: Sutter's bedroom, a kitchen, and a crude blacksmith's shop. His plans for a grander dwelling would have to wait for another year until he was eligible to acquire Mexican citizenship, and secure title to the land.

Much has been written about John Sutter. This is the account of the world-renown fortress he built, not the man himself.

Today the imposing walled compound of Sutter's Fort sits on two full Sacramento city blocks bounded by Twenty-sixth and Twenty-eighth Streets and K and L Streets, rising above sloping, park-like lawns dotted with shrubs and trees. The State Indian Museum occupies a sliver of the grounds, nestled among towering, ancient oaks on K Street that have been standing there since long before Sutter's time.

The California State Indian Museum entrance, seen from the pathway circling the Fort's north side ponds. *Photo by Author.*

The whole is surrounded by commercial and residential buildings, a sprawling hospital and adjacent medical facilities, two churches, and busy city streets. This modern-times urban development partly explains why the Fort appears lower in elevation than one might suppose from reading descriptions in historical accounts. The knoll Sutter chose to build on was much higher in 1839, relative to its surrounding prairielands, than it is now. Some erosion, but also fill brought in for new construction as the city of Sacramento grew, plus grading done when the Fort was restored in the 1890s, have reduced the relative height upon which the structure stands.

The address is 2701 L Street, a location Sacramentans nowadays refer to as "Midtown." But when the walls of the Fort rose in the early 1840s, there was nothing else there. No streets, no other structures except Sutter's own outbuildings, no town.

In the heady years of the Gold Rush, when the city of Sacramento only two miles west was rapidly expanding, the location of the Fort was considered too far from the center of commerce. During that era, no graded streets or neighborhoods reached the environs of the Fort, although a few pioneer breweries sat near its eastern end. Today, the Pioneer Memorial Congregational Church stands on the other side of L Street, with a sign that reads "Established in 1849." The sign, however, commemorates the formation of the first congregation in September 1849 beneath the oak trees near the river, not the present building. In fact, the church's first building at Sixth and I Streets was destroyed in Sacramento's second major fire, in July 1854.

Sutter's Fort shares a similar past marked by destruction and reconstruction, though the Fort was reconstructed on its original site. Except for the two-story Central Building, the structure visitors see today isn't the original, and is substantially smaller than the one John Sutter built. Overwhelmed by the thousands who rushed in after the gold discovery, Sutter sold sections of the Fort piecemeal to persons who had no interest in preserving the property. When they left, vandals appropriated bricks and wooden gates and roofs for building materials elsewhere. By the mid-1850s, the once-solid compound was in shambles.

But this is getting ahead of the story, so let's turn back to the beginning.

WHY BUILD A FORTRESS?

The very word "fort" conjures an image of a heavily guarded military installation. Yet prior to the late 1840s, institutionalized U.S. military presence was non-existent west of the Missouri River. As John Sutter rode west in 1838, the far-apart structures he saw were trading posts which supported the declining fur trade, almost always *fortified* against Indian attack with high palisades, towers, and strategically-placed cannon peeking through looped openings—hence the designation *fort*.

Sutter must have intended to build a wall around his own fledgling trading post from the start, because the Sacramento Valley, far removed from California's established coastal communities, was potentially a dangerous place in 1839.

Although several were indeed friendly, the Native American Indians who lived in the interior vastly outnumbered Sutter and his little crew. Most of them, in the parlance of the day, were considered "wild"—feared as marauders and horse thieves who raided coastal settlements with some regularity. Some of them were resentful, earlier runaways from the once-thriving Franciscan missions. Others were individuals who were left adrift now that the Mexican government had recently secularized the mission system. Many were hostile, ready and willing to annihilate any intruder. Should they decide one day to drive him out, Sutter could not count on swift aid from afar. He planned to bring colonists from Europe and America, and most Americans—well aware of their country's many years of Indian wars on the frontiers—regarded Indians with anxious distrust.

High walls would give the impression of safety.

Also, events happening elsewhere meant that Sutter couldn't altogether dismiss the potential of attack someday from the Mexican government itself. Only three years earlier Texas had declared itself independent from Mexico, an act preceded and followed by bloody conflicts. Other nations, whose ships routinely sailed Pacific waters, coveted the province of California. California politics, in turmoil over constant friction with the Mexican motherland and bitter rivalry between various internal factions, was hardly stable. If the province should become an object of foreign intrigue, Mexican officials might cast suspicion on Sutter, who was not one of their own, naturalized citizenship notwithstanding.

In fact, the Pacific Coast clear up to Canada simmered with discontent. In the north—about a month's overland travel—England and the United States held joint ownership of the Oregon Territory, an arrangement that satisfied neither. It was not inconceivable that in due time the two nations might go to war over the issue.

All things considered, it was only prudent to copy the design of other, successful outposts: to erect imposing walls and place cannon at key points.

GETTING STARTED

Sutter had several small cannon, some muskets and ammunition. He still had one of the three vessels he had used to ascend the Sacramento River: a four-oared pinnace (a small boat from a larger ship) which he had purchased from a sea captain. Game was plentiful, but he had no cattle or horses, and his provisions would not last forever.

Immediately, he wrote to Don Ygnacio Martinez—whom he had already met and negotiated with at the latter's ranch on Suisun Bay—asking for the swift delivery of the agreed-upon livestock plus one more yoke of oxen, two milk cows, two or three old saddles, dried meat, beans, corn for seed, some wheat, and a bag of *Manteca* (lard). The letter was dated August 14, 1839. Sutter sent two Indians to deliver it, and to help guide Martinez's men back to his encampment. Six weeks later Martinez sent some dried meat, a bushel of beans and a tub of lard; but the livestock wasn't delivered until late October, short a few heifers and calves.

Meanwhile, news of this European intruder traveled fast. Two weeks after Sutter landed, his nearest neighbor—some seventy miles away—showed up to pay a call. He was John Marsh, an American who had arrived in California three years earlier, now the owner of a ranch near the foot of Mt. Diablo. Marsh, who presented himself as a doctor, but had no medical degree, inspected the tents and huts, the mosquito and amphibian-filled slough, and disdainfully dubbed the whole place "Sutter's Frog Pond." Over time Sutter and Marsh developed a mutually-wary, sometimes contentious, yet mostly friendly relationship.

Sutter and his employees explored their new neighborhood and applied themselves to cutting a path back to the landing place on the American River, where Sutter later erected a tannery. During that winter they also hacked out a road to the Sacramento River, where there was more promising anchorage for watercraft. From the south side of the Fort, this narrow road jogged through the woods from

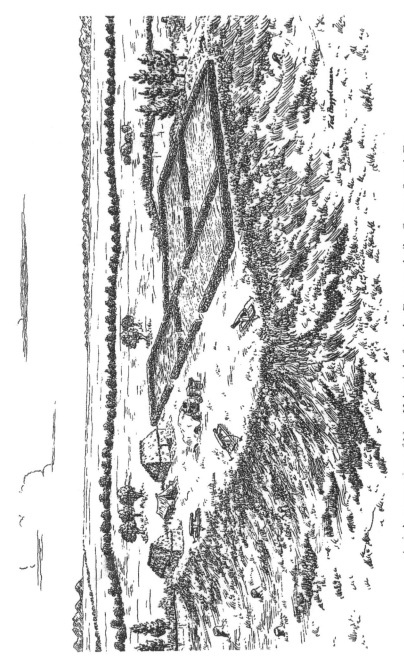

Artist's conception of New Helvetia before the Fort was built. *Courtesy Sutter's Fort.*

present-day L Street to about K and Fifth Streets, swerving again to end at the waterfront at the foot of J Street. This spot was Sutter's *embarcadero,* or landing place. There was no wharf, just a river sandbar that boats could be towed upon and secured to nearby trees with ropes.

Sutter next turned his attention to forming beaver trapping brigades, and organizing a fishing enterprise. Beaver pelts were a medium of exchange in barter-economy California. He planned to use them, as well as cured salmon, to buy tools and foodstuffs he needed to enlarge and sustain his little colony.

The Embarcadero (landing place) as sketched in October 1848. The view is to the east toward the future I Street in Sacramento. *Courtesy Sutter's Fort.*

Venison was the staple food, augmented by abundant wildfowl and the several varieties of fish that streamed through the rivers and creeks. Sweet, wild blackberries grew in profusion, but for a long time bread was a luxury. Just when other so-called soldiers of fortune (adventurous frontiersmen, and sailors who had jumped ship) began wandering in seeking jobs is unknown; Sutter later boasted that he had twenty white men in his employ by the end of 1840. He didn't have the cash with which to pay them, so their promised compensation was acreage and starter herds at some future time.

Sutter needed these men's expertise as carpenters or blacksmiths or hunters, and especially their help in training and supervising the Indians at a variety of tasks. And… his mandatory waiting period was about up. In late August 1840, Sutter traveled to Monterey where he took the oath to become a naturalized citizen of Mexico. Governor Juan Alvarado, beset by his citizens' complaints of Indian-perpetrated horse thievery, also commissioned Sutter as "the law" in the Sacramento District.

Now, Sutter was eligible to petition for a grant of land after meeting certain requirements. Among these were to erect some sort of permanent structure on the land, and to provide a *diseño*, a map of the desired grant's boundaries. He already had the little three-room house, and probably also, at that time, a small mudbrick-walled corral immediately east of it. In January 1841 Jean Jacque Vioget, another Swiss who had arrived in California two years before Sutter, and who had learned surveying during his career as a sea captain, provided the *diseño*.

Sutter's grant of nearly 50,000 acres—which stretched sixty miles northward from below the site of his outpost to the Sutter Buttes in a shape resembling the outline of a dinosaur thigh-bone—was formalized on June 18, 1841. One condition in the document specified that he bring twelve families to settle on the grant. He called his holdings New Helvetia, an archaic name for Switzerland.

Early Employees

Jared Sheldon. *Courtesy California History Room, California State Library, Sacramento.*

Among those twenty white men working for Sutter in 1840 was an English sailor named William Daylor, hired on as a cook. He was a friend and future partner of Vermont-born Jared Sheldon, who most likely came to the Fort in 1841.

A former schoolteacher and farmer, Sheldon was also a skilled carpenter. Soon after he arrived in California in March 1840, the Mexican government hired him to enlarge its Customs House in Monterey. He decided to take payment in the form of a land grant at some later date when he found suitable property.

In January 1844 Jared Sheldon received title to the Omochumney Rancho, 22,130 acres that straddled the Cosumnes River. Sheldon divided his grant with William Daylor, thereafter known locally as the

"Sheldon grant" in the western portion, and the "Daylor grant" in the eastern portion. On the north bank of the river Sheldon built a gristmill, the second one in the entire Sacramento Valley. It became fully operational in 1847. Three years later, as the Gold Rush escalated, he built a roadhouse he named The Slough House, which became a popular stage stop.

One of the many tragic casualties of the California Gold Rush, Sheldon was killed on July 12, 1851, by angry gold miners, for building an irrigation dam on his own property that flooded their upstream claims. He was buried next to his friend William Daylor, who had died of cholera the previous year.

BUILDING THE FORT, 1840-1841

Conventional building materials, such as those available in Europe or the United States, were scarce in California—but mud was everywhere, so the prevailing architecture in the province was adobe brick. In coastal regions this basic material was formed of a different sort of earth than that found near the American River. It was high in angular sand and gravel content, and the Spanish mission-builders, as well as the general home-building population, added straw to take up pore space because pore space that is too large can cause adobe bricks to crack and fail.

Sutter's mud came from a stream that had, for eons, coursed a hundred miles from the Sierra until the sediment load was beaten into microscopic clay particles known as the Ione Formation. This substance was rich in a mineral called kaolinite, a layered silicate mineral that has a low shrink-swell capacity, and bonds and compacts exceptionally well. He had no need to add straw, and in fact had none because his grain crops were not in full production. Technically, then—even though Sutter himself and his contemporaries described his structure as made of adobe—the Fort's building blocks were actually sun-dried, silicate-infused mud brick, a stronger and more durable material than traditional adobe brick.

Thousands of bricks had to be made, and to make them hundreds of men had to be employed, labor that fell to as many Indian teams as Sutter could hire through their chiefs. In brick construction, uniformity is important. Moistened earth was pressed and molded into an open timber frame, which was removed after initial setting, and the brick left to dry for several hours.

Sutter and his hirelings must have had to eyeball the knoll's parameters and contours, sketch a rough plan only to re-draw and try again, painstakingly measure and stake, and dig deep furrows for the foundation. Nineteenth century tools were rudimentary, yet not necessarily inefficient: a compass to set the direction of a Gunter's Chain (a device measuring sixty-six feet long, usually with a hundred swiveled links), as well as plumb lines and framing squares.

A mud brick from the Fort's original construction, on display in the Orientation Room. *Photo by Author.*

Did Sutter pattern his fortress after another he'd seen? Certainly, he had stopped at a few such installations on his way west in 1838. We have no answer, yet speculation persists.   Archeological excavation has so far failed to find the complete outline of the original Fort, but other sources confirm that Sutter's efforts produced an irregular rectangle. Sutter's own notes from the 1840s are lost or destroyed, but we can follow the building phases through the eyes of some of his visitors.

On August 17, 1840, before Sutter left for Monterey to become naturalized, a small group of would-be settlers, all men, arrived by land from Bodega Bay. They had come down the coast from Oregon by ship, then decided to continue southeast by land, hoping to avoid arrest by Mexican authorities. Their names were Peter Lassen, William Wiggins, Sebastian Keyser, Niklaus Allgeier, and Pablo Guitiérrez. At Sutter's they saw Hawaiian-style huts, where the Islanders and a few fur trappers lived, and Sutter's one-story, three-room mudbrick house. Native New Yorker Wiggins noted that Sutter's only protection was this tule-roofed dwelling, where he kept a brace of pistols on a table.

Once begun, though, work on a larger house advanced fairly rapidly, as reported by several visitors who showed up in 1841.

Late July 1841, Captain Phelps

A native of Gloucester, Massachusetts, William Dane Phelps went to sea as a cabin boy at an early age. By 1840 he was master of the 398-ton merchant trading ship *Alert*, making a series of trips between San Diego and Yerba Buena (San Francisco) to collect hides and tallow from California ranchers, and to sell them manufactured goods brought from New England.

On February 3, 1841, he met John Sutter in Yerba Buena cove and had dinner with him aboard the *Alert*. Sutter invited his new friend to come up and see his settlement in the Sacramento Valley, but Phelps's obligations in the hide and tallow trade took him down the California coast for several months. At last returning north, Captain Phelps left the *Alert* on July 27, 1841, in a boat with four hands and a pilot. Thanks to his sailing skills and strong southwest winds in going up the Sacramento River, he reached New Helvetia July 29, 1841.

Captain William Dane Phelps.
Author's collection.

Sutter was still living in his three-room house, but had commenced building a larger one before securing his land grant only the previous month. It is unclear from Phelps's journal whether he indeed saw the rising bastions, or merely noted Sutter's intent.

> *Found 100 Indians at work, some making dobys for building the walls of houses, others spreading them in the sun to bake, & others carrying those that are sufficiently hardened to the builders... In a square of about 200 feet Captain S. had a large three story house nearly finished for his own use. The square is to be enclosed by a doby wall 18 feet high & 4 thick, this wall forming the back part of the houses and shops of his artificers such as carpenters, blacksmiths, coopers, etc. Those houses... will all be enclosed, together with a horse & cattle corral.*

> *The enclosure as "Presidio" is to be fortified by two bastions at right angles commanding the wall in all directions with a shifting gun... thus he will in a few weeks be fortified at all points... The Presidio walls are fast rising, and will be finished in about a month.*

A deep gully lies near his house, which is partly filled with water and which by excavating about ¼ of a mile at each end and by a little cleaning out will bring the water from the American Fork to run by his door... This he contemplates doing, and at the same time he will not only be enabled to bring his boats near to his house, but will also have a fine site for mills.

His coal burners were at work felling trees and chopping off the limbs to make charcoal. We also passed by an extensive field enclosed for wheat by a fence. I should think about three miles in length, the longest fence I recollect seeing in any part of the world.

The nearly-finished large house was the long-enduring Central Building, always so-called even though it was placed west of center. The water-powered mills Sutter hoped to build never materialized, but Phelps's comments about the fence are interesting. Later guests saw deep ditches, not fences, protecting grain fields from roving livestock.

After enjoying a two-day elk hunt, Phelps departed August 3 for his ship, but this time conditions were less favorable and he did not reach the *Alert* until August 8. Six days later, on August 14, 1841, the U.S.S. *Vincennes*, under the command of Lieutenant-Commander Cadwalader Ringgold, USN, arrived in San Francisco Bay.

Charcoal was critical to the Fort's several manufactories because coal wasn't available naturally. Luckily, the wood of the native White Alder made excellent charcoal, which the blacksmiths used for their forges.

Ringgold and his vessel were part of the Wilkes Expedition, at present split into three factions because of severe problems encountered on the Oregon coast. Invited aboard, Phelps informed the naval officers of his visit to Sutter's establishment. Wanting to explore the interior and visit New Helvetia himself, Ringgold left with a large entourage in six boats, and provisions for thirty days. They landed near the Fort on August 23, 1841, departing two days later to explore the upper Sacramento River and its tributaries.

Another faction of the Wilkes Expedition, led by Lt. George Emmons, traveled overland from Oregon. This company arrived at the Fort October 19.

August-September-October 1841, the Wilkes Expedition

Sutter's settlement was only a minor object of interest to a major four-year scientific exploration that sailed around the world, sighted Antarctica (but didn't land there); visited South American ports, Australia, several Pacific islands, and the Pacific Northwest coast. Sparse field notes by expedition members (consolidated and condensed here) corroborate Captain Phelps's observations: "Sutter's establishment consists of a large adobe building now nearly finished, near which are others of smaller dimensions for workshops and dwellings… he is now fortifying the place by building a clay, or doby, fort at the opposite corners of a square enclosure of the same material."

Joel P. Walker.
Author's collection.

Significantly, Lieutenant Emmons' party of about twenty-five seamen and scientists brought the first American family to Sutter's Fort, Oregon émigrés from the previous year who attached themselves to the naval exploring party for protection. This was Joel Pickens Walker from Missouri. He was a brother of famed mountain-man/fur-trapper Joseph R. Walker, who would guide the wagons of the Joseph Chiles Party into California in 1843.

In October 1841 Joel Walker's family consisted of his wife Mary and their five children, the youngest born in Oregon in January 1841, and Mrs. Walker's unmarried sister Martha Young. They didn't stay long at the Fort. Sutter engaged Joel Walker to develop his new Hock Farm on the Feather River, a strictly agricultural venture named in honor of an Indian tribelet who lived in the area, "Hock" being

Sutter's interpretation of the name the Indians called themselves. Later, Joel was dispatched to Bodega to help bring down the Fort Ross livestock. In the spring of 1842, the Walker family moved on to the Napa Valley and eventually returned to Oregon, but came back to California during the Gold Rush.

Joel was adamant that they arrived at Sutter's Fort on October 22, and was so proud of the fact that his wife was the first American woman to come to the Fort that he engraved the date on her tombstone.

When Commander Charles Wilkes published his massive report in 1845, his descriptions of Sutter's Fort were minimal.

Mary Walker was the first pioneer woman to appear at Sutter's Fort, two months ahead of Bartleson-Bidwell Party member Nancy Kelsey. Mrs. Walker is buried in Healdsburg, Sonoma County. The inscription on her grave-stone reads: "Sacred to the memory of Mary wife of J.P. Walker who crossed the plains in 1840. Arrived at Sacramento October 22, 1841 died August 15th, 1856 aged 56 years."

His buildings consist of extensive corrals and dwelling houses, for himself and [his] *people, all built of adobe.* [Many of his stock can be seen] *around his premises, giving them an appearance of civilization. Captain Sutter has commenced extensive operations in farming; but in the year of our visit the drought had affected him and ruined his crops.*

The mountains to the east are visible from Captain Sutter's establishment.

Connected with the establishment, Captain Sutter has erected a distillery, in which he makes a kind of pisco from the wild grapes of the country.

This is the first mention of a still at the Fort. Probably this was a sort of jury-rigged contraption, because when Captain Phelps, a temperance man, revisited in March-April 1842, he tried to dissuade Sutter from erecting a distillery that Phelps says Sutter was "only thinking about" building at that time. Nonetheless, according to Sutter's own words, he did install genuine distillery apparatus in late

1843 or early 1844. He purchased the still equipment in 1843 from one of his usual creditors Antonio Suñol, a prosperous San Jose merchant and rancher. Born in Barcelona, Suñol had been living in California since 1818.

The distilling equipment seen today against the north wall is the same type of apparatus that Sutter installed. *Photo by Author.*

As for the Emmons party, even fewer words in the Wilkes Report are devoted to this detachment which, along with the settlers who accompanied them, arrived in a state of exhaustion after suffering sickness and hunger en route. Though scant in detailed information, Commander Wilkes did state the following:

> *I cannot avoid again returning my thanks to Captain Sutter for his kindness to this party. All the officers spoke most particularly of the attention he paid to them… and of his care and watchfulness in making provision for our sick.*

Wilkes's gratitude was prophetic. Hundreds of overland emigrants came to view Sutter's Fort as an end-of-journey destination, a haven for the truly destitute who had lost family members and possessions, as well as for those who were merely trail worn and weary.

September 1841, Count de Mofras

Today he would probably be arrested as a spy. Born in Toulouse into an aristocratic French family, Eugène Duflot de Mofras was educated as a botanist. He entered his country's diplomatic service, and in the late 1830s became an attaché of the French legation to Mexico. By order of his government, he left his post in Mexico City in 1839 to explore and document conditions and resources on the west coast of mainland Mexico, Alta and Baja California, and the Oregon Territory—all under the guise of gathering information to further French business interests.

It is now believed that his true mission was to assess possibilities for a French conquest. Mofras was thirty-one when he sailed upriver from the port at Yerba Buena to inspect the growing new colony at New Helvetia.

> *On the north, the fort of New Helvetia adjoins a small stream whose steep sides form a natural defense. The property is also surrounded by a wall five feet thick, built of sun-dried bricks, strengthened by heavy timbers, each side of the quadrangle being protected for a distance of 100 meters. The corners are flanked by square bastions two stories high, whose four surfaces are pierced with openings, while an outside gallery tops the entire wall.*

> *In the center of his fort, Mr. Sutter has constructed a few houses. The largest... is extremely well-built.*

Mofras was incorrect about the thickness of the walls (only the bastion walls were five-feet thick), and could not have seen the completed structure he described in such detail in his later-written report.

The spy was most interested in Sutter's armaments and maneuvers.

Equipment consists of 16 or 18 small cannons, carronades [short, smooth-bore, large-caliber cannon used from the 1770s by the British Royal Navy] *of various sizes purchased from ships, and two fine bronze fieldpieces procured by Mr. Sutter from the Russians. In addition he has... enough guns and rifles to arm 60 or 80 men...*

Active watches, including guards and night patrol, have been organized, for during the first years of this establishment the Indians upon several occasions attempted to assassinate Mr. Sutter... who has finally succeeded in keeping peace with them [and] *now has 100 natives in his employ. New Helvetia houses at the present time 30 white men, including German, Swiss, Canadians, Americans, Frenchmen and Englishmen. The majority are engaged in cutting wood, operating forges, or in carpentry.*

Eugène de Mofras spent a month off and on at New Helvetia, while he explored other aspects of the region and paid a visit to influential Mariano Vallejo at Sonoma. He and French-speaking Sutter got along famously, spending many evenings in spirited discussion. Mofras, who opined in his report that "Anyone with 200 guns could take California," departed the Fort convinced that his host supported a take-over by the French.

November-December 1841, the Bartleson-Bidwell Party

They were enticed to California in part on the strength of eyewitness reports from a Santa Fe trader named Roubideaux, and enthusiastic promotional letters published in Missouri newspapers. One of these was written by Sutter's first American visitor John Marsh, who hoped to attract new settlers in order to raise the value of his own property. Marsh didn't reveal his motives, of course—his words were crafted to create a vision of unlimited opportunity in his readers' minds. Excitement spread; a group of Missourians organized the Western Emigration Society. Among them was John Bidwell, who had lost his land in Platte County to a claim-jumper.

The Society attracted about five hundred persons eager to go to California, but just sixty-nine intrepid travelers showed up at the designated rendezvous point in May. The group named John Bartleson as their captain because Bartleson, accompanied by seven or eight men they couldn't afford to lose, refused to go otherwise. John Bidwell was elected secretary.

None knew the way. The greenhorns sensibly joined a company of Catholic missionaries headed for Flathead Indian territory, under the guidance of mountain-man Thomas Fitzpatrick. The route passed over much of what even then was called the Oregon Trail; however, Fitzpatrick was only going as far as Soda Springs in southeastern Idaho. Here, the missionaries swung north and the Bartleson party—now reduced to sixty-four in number by one accidental death and four who decided to return home—faced the unknown without a guide. Half of them opted to follow the missionary party north to Fort Hall and thence west into Oregon.

The rest—thirty-two men, one woman and a two-year-old girl—held firm to their resolution of going direct to California. Their journey was dangerous, exhausting, and frightening: days spent breaking wagon roads through sagebrush, days spent without water; days spent lost altogether.

Deciding to abandon their wagons near the Nevada-Utah border, the group fashioned pack-saddles for their draft animals and horses. They missed finding the Truckee River, the best ingress into California. Continuing south through the Nevada desert, they killed and ate the last ox while ascending the mountains somewhere north of the Sonora Pass. John Sutter became aware of their existence when James "Jimmy" John, who had become separated from the others, somehow found his way to the Fort. Sutter immediately sent food-laden pack mules with two Indians, who were unable to locate the party. Instead, Indians who worked for John Marsh found them in the San Joaquin Valley and guided them to Marsh's Rancho Los Meganos, where they arrived on November 4, 1841.

Here, though, the half-starved, bone-weary immigrants experienced less than a hospitable welcome from parsimonious Doctor Marsh. Following an unhappy episode in a Monterey jail while trying to obtain Mexican passports, a thoroughly disgusted Bidwell and three of his trail companions traveled eight days through pouring rain to reach Sutter's Fort, where they were warmly received. Toward Christmas the Kelseys—Benjamin, Nancy, and their young daughter—made it to the Fort by boat.

In his later writings Bidwell recorded the date of his arrival at Sutter's as November 28, 1841, and said that the building of the Fort had not yet begun, but was merely a "station" for the convenience of hunters and fur trappers.

The Bartleson-Bidwell Party was the first organized group of settlers to cross the Sierra Nevada. Miraculously, they all survived. Some of the men became prominent in the development of California: John Bidwell, Josiah Belden, Charles Weber, Joseph B. Chiles, and Michael Nye, among others. Another member of the company, a man calling himself Talbot Green, likewise achieved success until 1851, when a more recent immigrant recognized him as Paul Geddes, wanted in Philadelphia for embezzlement.

It is thought that the 1841 "eye-witness" testimonies of Phelps, Mofras, and the Wilkes Expedition all reflect elements of Sutter's future plans (especially their remarks about the bastions) and not what the individuals really saw.

None of them mention a gristmill, although Sutter is quoted as saying he had a gristmill in operation in 1840. We don't know when Sutter constructed the first "beehive" baking oven, probably during his first full year at his settlement.

These crude kitchen appliances (essentially a brick chamber constructed of indigenous clays and shaped like a dome), used in Europe from the Middle Ages, were common throughout the United States and other coun-

The frontier-style *horno* oven, used today to bake cookies & breads. *Photo by Author.*

tries during this era. Beehive ovens were sometimes built inside detached bake houses in New England, or out of doors in more temperate climates. Typically, the beehive oven took two to three hours to heat. Breads, cakes and pies were baked first, when the oven was hottest, followed by muffins and biscuits as it cooled. Pots of beans were often placed in the back of the oven to cook slowly overnight. In Mexican California these ovens were called *hornos*, or *hornitas*. The Fort's *horno* was outside in the east courtyard.

Yet even if the bastions and walls were still absent certain necessities were in place, and the Central Building was completed by the late summer or fall of 1841. In time Sutter's first three-room building housed a butcher shop, a combined straw-hat and shoe manufactory, and someone else's living quarters.

Fantasy: A Wilkes Expedition sketch of a fortress they could not have seen in 1841. *Courtesy Sutter's Fort.*

December 1841, the Russians

Since 1812 the Russians had owned an agricultural, and sea otter-hunting, outpost north of Bodega Bay they called Fort Ross. By the mid-1830s the California sea otter population was in serious decline, and Russian expectations of growing enough foodstuffs there to support their main colony at Sitka, Alaska, had proved disappointing. They decided to withdraw, and liquidate.

Offers extended to the British and French were turned down. Overtures to the Mexican government were rebuffed. The Mexican view was that the Russians were mere squatters in *their* territory and, by extension, every stick of local wood used in the improvements belonged to them, too. Why buy what they already owned? Mariano Vallejo, the powerful *comandante general* of the northern district, offered $9,000 for the livestock. The Russians felt they could get more.

In early September 1841, Alexander Rotchev, governor of Fort Ross, offered to sell John Sutter all of the Russian holdings at Ross, its outlying ranches, and the port at Bodega Bay. The price was stiff but Sutter, in desperate need of tools, lumber, and a host of other items with which to improve and equip his own settlement, accepted. The formal agreement, however, was delayed for three months while Sutter scrambled to raise the required cash down payment of $2,000. He and Peter Kostromitinov, the Russian-American Company's agent, signed the papers on December 13, 1841. The assets Sutter gained and the effect they had on Sutter's Fort will be discussed in the chapter titled "1841: The Fort Ross Purchase."

JOHN BIDWELL

John Bidwell had just turned twenty-two when he arrived at the Fort in 1841, and Sutter hired the intelligent, well-mannered former schoolteacher on the spot.

From January 1842 to March 1843 Bidwell was at Fort Ross, overseeing the dismantling of many buildings and the transport of its valuable lumber, plus livestock and other goods, back to Sutter's Fort. For about a year during 1843-1844 he was the foreman at Sutter's Hock Farm on the Feather River, and afterward Sutter's trusted clerk at the Fort. He accompanied Sutter on the 1845 Micheltorena campaign, and helped Sutter survey and lay out the town of Sutterville in 1846. Despite their age difference, the two developed a warm, affectionate, mutually respectful relationship that lasted the rest of their lives.

John Bidwell in 1850.
Courtesy California History Room, California State Library.

After becoming naturalized in 1844, Bidwell received a two-league land grant in Rio Vista, the Rancho Los Ulpinos, and another in Colusa, but disposed of both. He played a small part in the 1846 Bear Flag Revolt and served as a commissioned officer in the Mexican-American War. Discharged in 1847, Major Bidwell returned "home" to Sutter's Fort. Following Marshall's gold discovery at Coloma in 1848, Bidwell was the first to find rich gold deposits on the North Fork of the Feather River, founding a gold camp named Bidwell's Bar. His new-found wealth enabled him to purchase the 28,000-acre Rancho Del Arroyo Chico not far from his mine.

In 1849 he was elected to the State Senate for one year, traveling to Washington, D.C. to lobby for statehood. Back home he switched from mining to ranching, building up his new property with vineyards, fruit trees, grain fields, and livestock. Like almost all of the other farmer-ranchers of this period, he primarily used Indian labor. By 1853 he was growing so much wheat that he built a water-powered gristmill. He pioneered the production of casaba melons, olive oil, and dried fruits and nuts, as well as the utilization of a huge grain harvester drawn by forty mules.

During the Civil War he served in the California state militia and was appointed a brigadier general. In 1864 he was elected to the Congress of the United States for a two-year term and in 1866 unsuccessfully ran for governor of California on the Union Party ticket.

He married Annie Kennedy, the daughter of a high-level Washington, D.C. official, in 1868. Both were committed to social reform, in particular the welfare of the Indians, and the development of California's agricultural resources. In 1892 Bidwell was the National Prohibitionist Party nominee for president of the United States. He lost, but received more votes than any other Prohibitionist candidate had garnered in the past. Born in New York August 5, 1819, but raised in Pennsylvania and Ohio, John Bidwell died at his California ranch on April 4, 1900, a man of considerable reputation and integrity to the end. He had no children. John Bidwell is the founder of Chico, California.

NANCY KELSEY

Eighteen-year-old Nancy Kelsey trod two thousand dangerous miles from the border of American civilization at the Missouri River, holding her two-year-old daughter Martha Ann in her arms for much of the way while pregnant with a second child. Her husband Benjamin, whom she had married at age fifteen, was intent on finding better opportunities in the West. Nancy went along because she said she would rather endure the hardships of such a journey than the anxieties of an absent husband.

Nancy Kelsey. *Courtesy California History Room, California State Library.*

She was right about the hardships. Thirst, hunger, fatigue, and constant anxiety, especially after the company turned southwest from Soda Springs without a guide, plagued every mile. Party member Nicholas "Cheyenne" Dawson later described the scene after the company abandoned their wagons at the Utah-Nevada border: *I looked back and saw Mrs. Kelsey a little behind me, with her child in her arms, barefoot and leading her horse—a sight I shall never forget.*

Nancy made it over the deserts and mountains, and down the treacherous canyons of the Stanislaus River, before she finally collapsed in front of her distraught husband. Ben found game to revive his starving wife and the family continued on with the others to the home of John Marsh—who must have been quite surprised to see a young woman and child among a company of trail-toughened men. But Marsh's obstinate ways and still-primitive abode was no haven for a pregnant mother, so Ben and Nancy followed John Bidwell's lead to Sutter's establishment.

On Christmas Day 1841, Nancy gave birth at Sutter's Fort to a son who only lived for a few hours. The couple had nine more living children as they roamed to Oregon and back... drifting through the Napa Valley, El Dorado County, Humboldt County and Kern County with a sojourn into Mexico before settling in Texas in 1861. Migrating west again, they lived in Fresno County for a while before moving south to Los Angeles. They lived hardscrabble lives, rarely destitute but never financially secure.

Benjamin Kelsey died in Los Angeles County in 1889. Now aged 65, Nancy moved one last time, to a cabin about sixty miles east of Santa Maria, not far from one of her married daughters. She died there of cancer on August 10, 1896, just before her seventy-third birthday. She is buried near where her cabin stood, on what is now private property.

Nancy Kelsey was the first American woman to cross the Sierra Nevada.

1841: THE FORT ROSS PURCHASE

The sale price was $30,000, payable over a four-year period beginning in September 1842. For the first three years payment was to be made in country produce: wheat, peas, beans, soap, lard, and tallow, "all of the best quality." In the fourth year, the final payment was due in $10,000 cash—doubtless more coin than was in circulation in California when the agreement was signed.

The debt was staggering, even allowing for the scarcity of board lumber in the province, Sutter's real need for that item, and the many other articles he acquired. Worse, The Russians demanded a mortgage on New Helvetia to ensure payment, as delineated in Article IX: *His establishment on the Sacramento River, called New Helvetia... with all the goods moveable and immovable which thereto belong, shall be considered as a guarantee.*

What did Sutter receive in this deal and how did it affect the Fort?

- A square fort surrounded by 1,200 foot-long, 14 foot-high wooden posts with turrets in two corners; and, historians speculate, the chapel bell.
- A number of wooden dwellings containing heavy beams and wood-framed glass windows. Also sheds, shacks, barracks, fences, corrals, bath houses and warehouses. Fifteen kitchens, some containing stoves.
- Livestock: 1,700 head of cattle (oxen and cows), 940 horses, and 900 sheep.
- Machinery and equipment: plows and harrows; multiple harnesses, bridles and saddles. Saddle blankets, five four-wheeled carts, 10 two-wheeled carts, and 15 pairs of wheels, plus assorted scythes and sickles and several planked threshing floors. A machine for making cordage. Dairy equipment, two windmills, and blacksmithing equipment.

- Two horse mills (animal-powered gristmills).
- Furnishings: many tables and chairs, four armoires, six spring-roller shades, one bed mattress, and some cushions and sheets.
- Several boats, including two hide-covered launches, a *bidarka* [kayak], a long boat, and a 25-ton schooner "well suited for navigating all along the coast of California."
- An orchard with more than 260 fruit trees: apple, peach, pear, quince and cherry.

The dismantling and transfer of the Fort Ross and environs' moveable assets took almost two years to complete.

The wood from the Ross settlements was used to fashion posts, doors, and gates for the Fort. The glass windows were installed in the Central Building and elsewhere, and for years the toll of the chapel bell (if indeed the bell came from Fort Ross) called employees to work. Possibly one of the two horse mills, or parts of both, became improvements to the mule-powered gristmill Sutter installed near the northwest bastion. This meant he could grind his own wheat, thus reducing the cost of buying flour, and allowed him to produce ship's bread (hardtack), another item he used for trade. During harvest seasons the gristmill operated day and night, with a change of mules every four hours.

None of the items Sutter acquired were new, but undoubtedly the kitchen equipment was useful and the blacksmithing equipment put to good use. Having ready-made carts freed the carpenters for other tasks, and the furnishings were most welcome. Sutter renamed the 25-ton schooner the *Sacramento*. Having a larger vessel meant a faster voyage, and more tonnage hauled up or down river on each trip, saving time. About one hundred cattle drowned while being driven south, but this was no disaster because their valuable hides were stripped off the carcasses. Other assorted goods went with the sale, among them old uniforms the Russians wished to discard. These were given to Sutter's select private Indian guards, instilling pride in them and a greater motivation to protect the compound.

On the downside, the Russian plows proved too complicated for the Indians to use. The threshing floors were too tightly made to dismantle, and attempts to tow them behind the *Sacramento* resulted in their total destruction. The winnowing machine didn't work very

The functioning gristmill at Sutter's Fort still makes flour for demonstrations.
Photo by Author.

well. Few of the orchard trees survived transplanting, although John Bidwell did make cider from the apples.

In the space of a few months, Sutter had taken on two commitments he must honor, or fail. He must bring twelve families to settle on his land to validate his land grant, and he must pay the Russians in full to reclaim his title on mortgaged New Helvetia. Therefore his priorities turned to agricultural production, and promoting immigration. Sutter remained confident, trusting in future weather conditions (never a sure thing) to produce bountiful crops. He was certain that the final cash payment would materialize from expanded activities his newly acquired resources now made possible. For in addition to fulfilling that twelve-family requirement, incoming settlers would purchase his manufactured goods like shoes and hats and flour; and pay for the services of his blacksmiths, carpenters, and other skilled employees.

And there was another, unexpected benefit—a twist-of-fate by-product of the transaction. Far more important than acquiring *things*, Sutter's purchase of Fort Ross bought time. Time for Sutter's Fort to develop into the important, self-sufficient trading post it became, because as early as 1841 John Sutter's habitual delays in paying his many California creditors, combined with his often arrogant bluster, had offended some of the locals to the point of outright hatred. They wanted him gone.

Be that as it may, the Russian bill of sale was scarcely signed and celebrated before Governor Juan Alvarado and his uncle Mariano Vallejo knew every detail.

Having expected the assets of the Fort Ross colony to fall into their laps, they were furious. Sutter's brazen action was a slap in the face, an affront to them and their countrymen. Yet... there was that mortgage... if John Sutter disappeared or otherwise defaulted, would the Russians then move into the nascent settlement, threatening the safety of resident Californios and their far-off government in Mexico City? After all, Sutter's Fort occupied a strategic location right in the path of overland travel in all directions.

Mexican officialdom was well aware that several foreign nations coveted the province, and knew they lacked the resources to thwart a military takeover. At least, for the present, the Russians were leaving and they thought they knew the limitations of this particular Swiss foreigner.

They decided, however uneasily, to let him be.

The consequences of Sutter's rash purchase would not surface for seven more years, when another event jolted the Russians into reinforcing their sluggish efforts to collect on a four-year contract with more aggressive tactics. In the interim, Sutter and his trading post grew in status and influence—if at times hitting snags on a rocky path.

BUILDING THE FORT 1842-1846

March-April 1842, Captain Phelps Returns

The environmental conditions Captain Phelps (and the Wilkes Expedition) observed in 1841 changed dramatically only one year later. From the extreme of being so dry as to wither Sutter's field crops, excessive rainfall had so swelled the Sacramento and American Rivers that they overflowed into adjacent areas. Phelps could only reach the Fort via kayak, manned by Hawaiian Islanders, through water so high that he disembarked just below its walls. This time he recorded nothing about the structure but did appreciate the Fort's agricultural production and increase in livestock.

> *Everything looks well and thriving. Owing to his want of seed he will not have a great variety of garden stuff, or near the quantity of field produce he* [would have had otherwise]. *However, he has now 300 acres of wheat growing in one field, also about 160 acres of rye, beans, and potatoes.*

> *The kitchen garden* [on the north side of the slough]... *has 5 or 6,000 grape vines planted this year, fruit trees, and a good variety of salad radishes, leeks, and strawberries. The livestock... now consists of 3,400 cattle, 500 milch cows, and 46 pairs of working oxen. Of horses* [there are] *1,500, of which 300 are saddle and working horses. Sheep, about 1,600; 40 mules, and 350 hogs.*

> *Considering that it is but about two years that Captain Sutter first arrived, he has done wonders.*

Good weather, of course, was a crucial factor in enabling Sutter to meet his obligations to the Russians and thereby reclaim title to his property. In 1842 he managed to make a partial payment on the $5,000 due that year in produce, but none the following year.

In 1843, capricious Mother Nature changed her mind again: the valley suffered a drought so severe the soil cracked, which brought New Helvetia's wheat crop to the brink of utter failure.

Summer 1843, Lansford Hastings

Hastings was a young Ohio lawyer who emigrated to Oregon Territory in 1842, where he helped establish Oregon City during the winter months. He was also an adventurous, far-sighted dreamer. Claiming that he hadn't ever intended to settle in Oregon permanently anyway, he agreed to lead a party south to California the following year. They left on May 30, 1843, arriving at Sutter's Fort July 10. In his party were James C. Coates, whom Sutter hired as a tanner; Nathan Coombs, John Daubenbiss, and Thomas Shadden.

Lansford W. Hastings.
Courtesy California History Room,
California State Library.

Shadden, a mule trader, was accompanied by his wife. It is not clear whether he worked at the Fort, but he was there many times over a two-year period, and lived somewhere along the Bear River, a tributary of the Feather. Daubenbiss, a miller by trade, soon moved on to San Jose but did join Sutter's troops for the 1845 Micheltorena campaign. Nathan Coombs, an eighteen-year-old from Massachusetts, took work with William Gordon, who owned a ranch in present-day Yolo County. He applied for Mexican citizenship in 1844, and married Gordon's daughter Isabella at the Fort the same year, with Sutter performing the ceremony. Coombs was in Sutter's army for the Micheltorena campaign, was present in Sonoma during the Bear Flag Revolt, and later joined the California

Battalion. In 1847 he purchased farmland in the Napa Valley, where he founded and laid out the city of Napa.

Lansford Hastings remained at the Fort off and on through the winter—presumably writing the first draft of his book—until the spring of 1844, when he sailed to Mexico, crossing it overland on his way home to Ohio.

One of the better descriptions we have of the early Fort is from Hastings' book *The Emigrants' Guide to Oregon and California*, written to promote emigration to the Far West, and published in 1845.

> *In form it is a sexangular* [hexagonal] *oblong, its greatest length being 428 feet, and its greatest width 178 feet; 233 feet of its length being 178 feet wide, and the residue but 129 feet wide. It is enclosed by permanent adobie walls, which are 18 feet high, and three feet thick, with bastions at the corners the walls of which are five feet thick. It is entered by two large swinging gates, one of which is on the north, another on the south side, and a third in the east end. The first of these is entirely inaccessible from without, because of a deep and impassible ravine, which extends the whole length of the fort on the north side; on each side of the second, is a platform upon each of which a nine-pounder* [cannon] *is planted, and the third is completely commandeered by one of the bastions.*

> *There are two bastions, each of which has four guns, two nine-pounders and two six-pounders; and in all, there are twelve guns, of different caliber. The inner building of this fort consists of a large and commodious residence for the various officers, in connection with which, is a large kitchen, a dining room, two large parlors, the necessary offices, shops and lodging apartments. Besides these, there is also a distillery, a horse mill and a magazine* [an ammunition storage and feeding device within or attached to a repeating firearm] *together with barracks, for the accommodation of, at least, one thousand soldiers.*

> *In connection with the Fort there are 1,000 acres of land, under a good state of cultivation… together with an extensive tannery.*

Hastings' travel guide indeed drew hundreds of overlanders to Sutter's Fort. His emphasis on the Fort's size and artillery was obviously meant to reassure potential settlers of their own safety in the Sacramento Valley. Other statements were to impress farmers with the quality of the soil and to assure future cattle ranchers that there was an available facility to process their hides for the profitable hide and tallow trade.

Some of his descriptions, however, require clarification. The entrances on the east and south sides were the ones with large swinging gates; the smaller north entrance only had a large door. The west side of the enclosure was wider than the east end because the north wall, instead of being a continuous straight line, was offset east of the Central Building to adjust for the contours of the slough.

November-December 1843, the Chiles-Walker Party

The arrival on November 10 of Joseph Chiles and his group of thirteen riders was definitely a boon to the Fort's workforce.

Chiles, a member of the 1841 Bartleson-Bidwell Party, had returned east in 1842 to bring more settlers to California, but this company had separated at Fort Hall because of food shortages. Joe Chiles led a group of single men on horseback who intended to live off the land until they reached Sutter's Fort. The wagons with the women and children, most of the food supplies, and the other men in the company, continued under the leadership of mountain man Joseph R. Walker.

The Walker-led contingent entered the province in early December 1843, around the southern end of the Sierra. These people, forced to abandon their wagons in the Owens Valley, had dispersed by the end of December and only a small segment arrived at Sutter's Fort the following January: George Yount's daughters Elizabeth and Frances, Frances's husband Bartlett Vines and their two children, William Baldridge, James "Old Wheat" Atkinson, and Mary Eyre, who married Sutter's neighbor John Sinclair.

Chiles and his followers entered California at its northeast corner, via the Malheur River. Riding with Chiles were William Winter, John Wooden, Milton McGee, and Thomas Westly Bradley. Also the four Williams brothers James, John, Squire and Isaac; and the new Fort Hall recruits Pierson B. Reading, Captain John Gantt,

Samuel J. Hensley, and possibly William Martin, an Oregon wagon train captain.

Joseph Chiles and his friend Billy Baldridge settled in the Napa Valley region in early 1844, but Pierson Reading, Samuel Hensley, John Gantt and the Williams brothers accepted employment at the Fort. Hensley became the supercargo (the agent in charge of the cargo, but not the ship) aboard Sutter's schooner *Sacramento*. And, for a time, he was the overseer at Sutter's Hock Farm.

Pierson Reading hired on as Sutter's head trapper. This was a management position better known in the fur trade as the *booshway*, a title that was a corruption of the French word *bourgeois*. John Gantt, a former Army captain turned fur-trapper, also joined Sutter's fur-trapping enterprise.

James Williams worked as a blacksmith; his brother John Williams worked as a tanner. Thomas Westly Bradley, a twenty-five-year-old Missourian, took on a variety of jobs at the Fort. He cut shingles, dug ditches, and cleared the headwaters of the slough to keep the water flowing. Undoubtedly his most enjoyable task was helping to place a bell in the Fort's courtyard, which afterward rang each half-hour to signal "all's well." Bradley remained until March 1844, when he found employment on George Yount's ranch in Napa Valley. That same year, all four Williams brothers settled in Santa Cruz.

In later years, Samuel J. Hensley became a prominent business-man in San Jose. Pierson B. Reading was the first American to establish residence in Shasta County. Reading's impressions of the Fort are as follows:

> *The fort itself is large and cozy on its approach, with its high walls, its bastions frowning with heavy cannon. It is the largest and best fortified fort in California. The walls encompass an area of about 400 feet square, and are built of sun-dried bricks. They are about three feet thick, 15 feet high, and defended by several large cannon planted in reversed bastions. A distillery for the distillation grain and the juice of the grape is in the yard, and in one corner is a mill for the grinding of wheat. There is also a blacksmith shop, a carpenter's shop and a shoe-maker's shop; and connected with the establishment is a tannery.*

March 1844, Lieutenant John Charles Frémont

John Charles Frémont. *Courtesy California History Room, California State. Library*

On March 6, 1844, Frémont, his guide Kit Carson, and his U.S. Topographical Engineers exploring company arrived at the Fort in considerable distress, famished and exhausted after their near-fatal crossing of the Sierra Nevada in severe winter conditions. Frémont and his followers remained encamped in the vicinity until March 22, to rest themselves while the Fort's employees re-supplied their needs. Frémont recorded:

We were in want of everything. Mules, horses, and cattle were to be collected; the horse-mill was at work day and night, to make sufficient flour; the blacksmith's shop was put in requisition for horse shoes and bridle bits; and pack-saddles, ropes, and bridles and all other little equipments of [our] *camp were again to be provided.*

The fort is a quadrangular adobe structure... capable of admitting a garrison of a thousand men; this, at present, consists of forty Indians, in uniform—one of whom was always found on duty at the gate.

The inner wall is formed into buildings comprising the common quarters, with a blacksmith's and other workshops; the dwelling house, with a large distillery-house, and other buildings, occupy more the center of the area.

From this we know that by the time of Frémont's arrival in March 1844, the interior walls were in place and partitioned into rooms with mud bricks or, in some cases, with moveable cowhide curtains. The distillery apparatus was installed and operative. Frémont also saw young Indian girls who were in training for a future woolen factory, but this enterprise wouldn't become a reality until the following year.

Summer 1844, the Kelsey Party (from Oregon)

Ben and Nancy Kelsey, who had driven some cattle up to Oregon's Willamette Valley to sell, returned to California. With them came several members of the Kelsey clan who had opted for Oregon back in 1841 when the Bidwell-Bartleson Party reached Idaho.

December 1844, the Stephens-Murphy-Townsend Party

On December 10, 1844, two women and four men rode into the Fort seeking help, followed a few days later by about thirty men. All were members of the Stephens-Murphy-Townsend Party, the first immigrants to bring wagons over the Sierra Nevada, albeit in incremental stages that took several months. Several of these overlanders eventually dispersed to coastal settlements. Some took jobs at the Fort, and Martin Murphy Junior, with his wife and family, established a ranch near today's Elk Grove. However, all of the above settling or relocating happened some months later in 1845.

Meantime, John Sutter somehow convinced a good number of the men who arrived in December 1844 to join his ranks in the infamous Micheltorena Campaign.

For sure John Sutter's worst lapse in judgment—one that might have ended the very existence of New Helvetia then and there had his captors not decided to pardon him—was his leading role in a military operation to defend Mexico City-appointed Governor Manuel Micheltorena against his rebelling California subjects. Sutter led his troops from the Fort on January 1, 1845, with high resolve and flying flags, but ultimately the rebels triumphed. Near Los Angeles, Micheltorena surrendered and Sutter was briefly taken prisoner. His cause defeated, he returned April 1—a bit shaken but still in charge of his settlement. During Sutter's absence Pierson Reading was in charge of the Fort.

Three months after Sutter's return, another party of immigrants arrived from Oregon.

July 1845, the McMahon-Clyman Party

In the spring of 1845, Green McMahon organized a company of fellow Oregon pioneers who wanted to give California a try, hiring former fur trapper James Clyman to guide them south. After a month's journey, on July 10 Clyman brought his charges safely to the Gordon Ranch on Cache Creek. Two days later, as Clyman noted in his journal, several members of this party "packed up and left for Captain Sutter's."

Clyman himself, having instead opted to ride off toward San Francisco Bay, didn't arrive back at the Fort until July 21. He thought it had an imposing appearance at a distance, standing on an elevated plain and surrounded by wheat fields—but on closer inspection discovered, to his disgust, that the entire structure was covered with dust and fleas.

Sutter was ecstatic to receive the immigrants. In his letter to U.S. Consul Thomas O. Larkin, Sutter enthused that "All of these people have a decent appearance and [there are] some very useful men among them. Some will remain here, and the majority will spread over the whole country like usual…"

The looms in the Fort's Weaving Room were constructed to replicate those that James Marshall built in 1845. *Photo by Author.*

As required, Sutter also sent a list of names and occupations to Thomas Larkin. Most of the thirty-nine immigrants listed were farmers, with a sprinkling of tradesmen. Farmer William Northgrave, blacksmith Allen Sanders, and saddler J.D. Perkey accepted jobs at the Fort. So did a coach maker and carpenter named James Wilson Marshall.

Jack-of-many-trades James Marshall was soon set to work making spinning wheels, looms, and shuttles; the essential equipment needed, but previously unobtainable, to commence a blanket factory at the Fort. We don't know when the first blanket was cut from the weaving apparatus, but clearly Marshall built more than one loom. This is evidenced in Sutter's letter dated November 5, 1845, to Pierson Reading at Camp Henishaw, the trapper's camp about a day's sail down the Sacramento River:

> *You are certainly doing very well, and no doubt it will continue so by your good management... for the present I can send you not more than 5 blankets as only one loom is going at present, until they are done with sheep shearing and washing the wool.*

Fall 1845, Overland Immigration

The 1845 immigration was the largest body of overlanders so far, and brought significant numbers of women and children. Among the best known groups was the large John Grigsby-William Ide Party composed of families and hired teamsters. William Ide, his wife Susan and their children, settled near Red Bluff. John Grigsby took his family to the Napa Valley, where he was hired by George Yount.

James and Eliza Gregson, her mother Anna Marshall, and Eliza's three siblings, were attached to this party. So were the Bonney brothers and their families, and William Elliot with his wife and seven children. Friends William Todd and William Swasey, leading a small party of about thirteen single men, had eschewed wagons in favor of faster pack-mules.

Straggling far behind the others that year was Lansford Hastings, returning to California after publishing his *Emigrants Guide* and traveling about on a whirlwind lecture tour. Leading a small party of mule-mounted men, he left the Missouri frontier in August. Among Hastings' party were William N. Loker of St. Louis, whom Sutter hired as assistant clerk at the Fort, and giant Robert Semple of Illinois, who stood six feet, eight inches tall. The following spring, Captain Sutter hired Semple to assist John Bidwell in finding a suitable site for a mill on the Feather River. The two agreed the area had potential, but after a protracted argument over the feasibility of floating milled boards downriver, Semple decided—perhaps in a huff—not to return to the Fort. He is best known to history as the founder of Benecia, and the co-founder of the first newspaper in California, the *Monterey Californian.*

The Swasey-Todd group, and the several wagon companies, arrived at Sutter's Fort between September 27 and October 25. In addition, brevet captain John Charles Frémont and his armed exploring party suddenly reappeared on December 10. Hastings's outfit, tempting fate with their late start, arrived at the Fort on Christmas Day.

Altogether the 1845 overland immigration amounted to some three hundred individuals, mostly Americans. Suspicion swelled in the hearts of Mexican officials, who now began to grow nervous. On November 11, 1845, a small contingent of Mexican officers, led by Comandante General José Castro, rode into the Fort to meet with Captain John Sutter. Accompanying Castro was Andrés Castillero from Mexico, who had government authorization to offer a purchase price of $100,000 for Sutter's Fort "with all its appurtenances." After consulting with four of his most trusted employees, Sutter declined the offer. Perhaps disappointed, Castro and Castillero accepted Sutter's decision and departed the next day. But trouble was brewing.

Dr. William Brown Gildea, a physician and dental surgeon, was one of the young single men with the Swasey-Todd Party. He studied medicine in St. Louis, Missouri, under the instruction of his uncle, Dr. B. B. Brown, and after graduating from St. Louis University in 1843, he decided to practice in California. At Sutter's Fort, Dr. Gildea was welcomed joyously as the first doctor in residence. Unfortunately, he contracted malaria and died at the Fort on January 24, 1846. He was 26.

June 1846, Dr. Marius Duvall

We might imagine that Sutter's Fort has always gleamed with whitewash, but not so. Earlier visitors saw drab mud-colored walls, and so did Dr. Duvall in 1846. Appointed as a naval Assistant Surgeon assigned to the U.S. sloop-of-war *Portsmouth*, Marius Duvall had occasion to visit Sutter's Fort June 14–17. Dr. Duvall, born and raised in the bosom of a privileged Maryland family, described the Fort in rather unflattering terms:

> *This gentleman's establishment consists of two or three acres of ground enclosed by mud walls about twenty feet in height; just outside them are several corrals of the same material, which at first sight seem to be a part of the fortification.*

> *The whole is unwhitewashed and of a very dirty appearance. His house is in the center of the enclosure, is extremely plain, its exterior and interior show that the owner has very little idea of comfort. There is not a tree near it.*

If comfort was lacking industry had increased, because in June 1846 the blanket factory was in full operation. Shown the spinning and weaving rooms, Dr. Duvall recorded what he observed—adult Indian men who had been trained at the missions doing the weaving, while several Indian women and girls picked and spun the wool.

Reports of the Fort as it was in Sutter's time, its dimensions and attributes, vary with the source. Adding to the confusion are these descriptions by Navy Lt. Joseph Revere in July 1846, and by Edwin Bryant, a journalist who arrived September 1, 1846.

> Revere: *The Fort consists of a parallelogram enclosed by adobe walls, fifteen feet high and two feet thick, with bastions or towers at the angles... there is a second wall on the inner face, the space between it and the outer wall being roofed and divided into workshops... also a well of good water.*

Bryant: *The fort is a parallelogram, about 500 feet in length and 150 feet in breadth.*

Sutter himself said that his outer walls were eighteen feet high, two-and-a-half feet thick, and enclosed 75,000 square feet.

After my return from Monterey I started to build a fort... I built a large house near the first adobe building... At two corners I built bastions with walls five feet thick; under these bastions were the prisons. Within the enclosure I erected other buildings; barracks, workshops and dwellings, a bakery, a mill, and a blanket factory. The tannery was built on the spot where I first landed. There were several outhouses for vaqueros and other employees... It took four years altogether to complete the fort.

When was the Fort completed? Eye-witnesses as well as modern researchers offer conflicting dates. The exterior walls were not in place when John Bidwell arrived in late November 1841, but they were when Bidwell's trail companion Joseph Chiles returned in early November 1843 with a new group of immigrants.

The Central Building was built first, then the two opposite bastions at the southeast and northwest corners, each approximately twenty-seven feet high. An outer wall rose to connect the bastions and surround an inner courtyard. When this was finished, the lower inner walls were put in place. Finally, the space between the walls was divided into separate rooms, and roofed. Somewhere in between, Sutter constructed separate mudbrick buildings inside the courtyard for a kitchen and distillery. Assuming Sutter counted 1841 as his start time—the year he received his land grant and built the Central Building—construction of the Fort was as finished as it was ever going to be by the end of 1845-beginning of 1846.

PIERSON B. READING

Pierson Barton Reading (pronounced *red-ding*) was one of the most prominent and respected men in early California. He was born in New Jersey on November 26, 1816, into a distinguished family that counted a Revolutionary War captain and a governor of New Jersey among its ancestors. Reading spent his boyhood in New Jersey, attending local schools. An ambitious youngster, he left home at age fourteen to seek his fortune. Eventually, he become a cotton broker in Mississippi and Louisiana.

That business failed when Reading's partner fled with embezzled monies, and in 1843 his young wife died. He decided to go west. His original goal was Oregon, but at Fort Hall, Idaho, he impulsively joined the California-bound Joseph Chiles Party.

Pierson B. Reading in 1862. *Courtesy of the Shasta Historical Society.*

Upon arrival at Sutter's Fort in November 1843, Reading quickly became one of Sutter's most trusted employees. First as a clerk for a short time, and then as Sutter's head trapper, an activity that allowed him to explore large sections of the Sacramento and San Joaquin Valleys. He became a Mexican citizen in 1844, and received a 26,632-acre land grant he named Rancho San Buenaventura. Extending nineteen miles along the west bank of the Sacramento River from Cottonwood Creek to Salt Creek, it was the northern-most Mexican land grant ever awarded.

Reading was an active participant in the June 1846 Bear Flag Revolt, joining the California Battalion when the Mexican-American War burst onto California soil three weeks later. Commissioned with the rank of major, he was one of the signers of the Treaty of Cahuenga in January 1847, which ended the fighting in California.

Among the first to visit Coloma after the gold discovery in January 1848, Reading returned north where he found a reported $80,000 in gold on Clear Creek, and on the Trinity River. By year's end he was a merchant, partnered with Samuel Hensley and 1845 immigrant Jacob Snyder. For a few weeks, Hensley, Reading & Company also counted John Sutter's son, August Sutter, as a fourth partner. The firm purchased mercantile space inside Sutter's Fort, where it operated until moving to burgeoning Sacramento City in mid-1849.

Upon statehood in 1850, Reading's Rancho San Buenaventura served as the first seat of Shasta County.

Reading was known as a man of character and integrity, and in 1851 his many admirers nominated him as the Whig candidate for governor of California. He narrowly lost, yet decided to eschew politics in favor of further developing his ranch. He raised cattle and cultivated grapes, olives, pears, grains, and vegetables. In 1862, he received an award from the California Agricultural Society for having the finest stock farm in the state. He died at his ranch on May 29, 1868, survived by his wife Fannie, whom he had married in 1854, and five children.

Although the modern city of Redding spreads across much of his former land grant, Redding, California, is *not* named for Pierson Barton Reading. That honor went to Benjamin B. Redding, an agent for the Southern Pacific when the railroad laid out the town site in 1872.

ELIZA GREGSON

Elizabeth Marshall Gregson was born in England March 24, 1824. She attended grammar school, and later worked in a cotton yarn factory in Hayfield. Eliza emigrated to the United States with her family in 1839, settling in Pawtucket, Rhode Island.

She met fellow British subject James Gregson, a trained blacksmith who had arrived in Philadelphia as a boy in 1837, and married him on October 20, 1843, when Eliza was nineteen.

Eliza Gregson. *Courtesy California History Room, California State Library.*

A year later the Gregsons moved to Illinois, where she gave birth to a son in 1844 who lived for only three months. Eliza had no desire to work in the Illinois cotton mills, and feared her husband "wasn't stout enough" for heavy blacksmith's work. Indeed, James had trouble holding a job because he was frequently ill, so they were always teetering on the brink of poverty.

By the spring of 1845 the couple, now sharing their home with and supporting Eliza's mother Anna Marshall and Eliza's three younger siblings, was destitute. They decided to go to Oregon, where they heard good free land was available. West of Fort Hall, Idaho, their six oxen began to fail—forcing them to cut down their wagon into a cart. This, in turn, meant abandoning many of their personal goods, including provisions and supplies. They joined another party as hired hands, but a few miles farther on they encountered the Grigsby-Ide Party, bound for California under the guidance of mountaineer Caleb Greenwood. Greenwood, who had been hired by John Sutter to divert emigrants into the Sacramento Valley, convinced the Gregsons to change their destination. Another disaster threatened along the Humboldt River, when they lost all but two oxen to Indian raids.

The Gregsons made it to Sutter's Fort on October 5, 1845. Sutter hired James, and Eliza's teenaged brothers, to whip-saw timber near the Cosumnes River. Eliza's mother Anna Marshall married Englishman James Smith at the Fort on January 11, 1846, taking Eliza's sister Mary Ann, and perhaps the younger brother, John, with her when she moved to Smith's farm. Henry Marshall, the oldest brother, stayed on at the Fort as an employee.

A few days after Anna Marshall's wedding James and Eliza accepted work with Thomas Hardy, another Englishman, at his ranch on the Sacramento River near Cache Creek. There, the couple lived in what Eliza called a "crude tule wigwam." They returned to the Fort in the spring of 1846, where Eliza lived while James first participated in the Bear Flag Revolt in June, and then a few weeks later enlisted in a volunteer battalion to fight in the Mexican-American War. At this time, other pioneering wives moved into the Fort for their own safety. To pass the time while waiting for their men's return from the war, Eliza taught reading and writing to Mrs. Daniel Leahy, Mrs. James McDowell, and Mrs. Allen Montgomery. On September 2, 1846, Eliza gave birth at the Fort to a daughter she named Ann.

After the gold discovery the Gregsons went to Coloma where James extracted $3,000 in gold, but became ill again in late 1848. The family, now enlarged by the birth of a second daughter, moved to Sonoma. Eliza supported her husband and children by taking in washing, ironing and sewing until James recovered his health. About 1850 they jointly purchased, with her brother Henry, a 160-acre farm in Green Valley.

At the first county fair in Healdsburg, Eliza and James received a silver butter knife for the best butter. The Gregsons were among the first to grow wheat successfully in this area and remained there the rest of their lives, raising a brood of eight healthy children. Eliza Gregson died February 1, 1889, aged 65; James lived on for another decade, dying in August 1899.

1846: THE BEAR FLAG REVOLT AND THE AMERICAN CONQUEST

B y the late spring of 1846—although General José Castro had as yet done nothing more overt than rattle his sword—rumors were rife among the new settlers that he intended to forcibly expel them from the province. Frightened, angry, and agitated, some of the settlers milled about Sutter's Fort while others rode north to the Sutter Buttes to confer with Captain John Charles Frémont, who had recently returned from a foray into Oregon. When Frémont refused to publicly lead them, a few took matters into their own hands.

Mariano Vallejo. *Courtesy California History Room California* State Library.

Before daybreak on June 14, a band of armed settlers galloped into the headquarters of Commandant General Mariano Vallejo in Sonoma, captured the town, and declared that California was now an independent republic. And they took prisoners: Mariano Vallejo, his brother Salvador, his secretary Victor Prudon, and his American brother-in-law Jacob Leese. A few days later Frémont swept in to take command, organizing the California Battalion to further the cause. Ironically, through all the drama surrounding the Bear Flag Revolt of June 14-18, no one in California knew that the United States had officially declared war on Mexico the previous May.

The new California Republic, with 1845 immigrant William B. Ide as its president, lasted less than a month. On July 7, 1846, Commodore John Drake Sloat, commanding the U.S. Navy's Pacific Squadron, seized the port of Monterey and raised the American flag over the Customhouse—whereupon José Castro and Governor Pio Pico fled the territory. The Mexican-American War had come to California soil, and with it America's conquering forces. On July 11, the Stars and Stripes was raised on the Fort's flagpole.

The impact of all this on Sutter's Fort was two-fold.

First: On June 16, Captain Frémont forced John Sutter to imprison the Bear Flaggers' captives—all of whom Sutter knew well—inside the Fort.

Second, on or about the same date, Frémont commandeered the Fort as an operations base for his California Battalion. He renamed it Fort Sacramento and put his own man, his expedition's artist and cartographer Edward "Ned" Kern, in charge, thus freeing himself to move up and down the coast to stifle resistance from the Mexican Californians. After Commodore Robert Stockton arrived to replace the ailing Commodore Sloat, the California Battalion operated with Stockton's full support. (Unfortunately for himself, Frémont threw in his lot with the wrong commander. The following year his rightful superior officer, U.S. Army General Stephen Watts Kearney—whose orders from Washington D.C. gave Kearney the top position in California—hauled him back to the nation's capital to face court-martial. For his questionable actions, and his defiance toward Kearny, Frémont was convicted of mutiny, insubordination and misconduct.)

Meanwhile, Sutter treated the Bear Flag prisoners kindly, installing them in his "best rooms" instead of the dank lockup beneath the southeast bastion. He ate dinner with them, played cards with them, and took walks with them in the evenings. Vallejo, and his relatives and friends, were finally released in early August by order of Commodore Stockton.

But Edward Kern remained in command at the Fort for months to come.

Entries in the *New Helvetia Diary*, the logbook of daily Fort activities, cease during this period of military occupation. Some have interpreted this silence as Sutter's humiliation at being relegated to underling status in his own establishment. Yet—making the best of an unpleasant situation—Sutter befriended Edward Kern, who was often ill, and corresponded with him for several years afterwards.

A more likely explanation is that Sutter was so frantically busy he didn't have time to record anything. After all, his clerks and a large number of his skilled tradesmen were gone: they had joined the California Battalion. A number of women and children had moved inside the walls for protection because no one could predict the duration or geographical extent of military engagement, and Sutter felt responsible towards them. Without the logbook as a reference, we must assume that the Fort's regular agricultural activities continued as usual, but perhaps on a reduced scale, and with many chores left undone. As things turned out the theater of war never reached the Fort, but there were steady requisitions for flour and beef to feed American troops.

At some point during the war, Sutter extended an offer to sell his trading post to the United States, at a price reportedly $20,000 lower than the one he had been offered by Mexican official Andrés Castillero in 1845. From the Americans' point of view, though, the mere occupation of the Fort served just as well as a purchase, and the matter was never a subject of serious discussion.

Sam Brannan Arrives

In the midst of all this turmoil, the 445-ton *Brooklyn*, six months and 24,000 sea miles distant from its departure at New York, dropped anchor in San Francisco Bay on July 31, 1846.

Aboard were more than two hundred men, women, and children. Nearly all of the passengers were of the Mormon faith, seeking a new home outside the jurisdiction of the United States where they might find refuge, and freedom from religious persecution. When they left New York on

The *Brooklyn*, from a painting by Duncan McFarlane. *Author's collection.*

February 4, the site of a permanent new home for the Latter Day
Saints had not yet been chosen. Mexican-owned California was but
one of several destinations under discussion, and they were surprised
and distressed to see an American flag fluttering in the breeze when
they landed. The weary travelers, who had buried twelve of their own
in watery graves in perhaps the longest religious sea pilgrimage in
recorded history, had no choice but to remain in California until told
by President Young where the Church would settle.

The sea-faring group's leader and voyage organizer was a twenty-
eight-year-old Mormon Elder named Samuel Brannan, a printer by
trade. The Saints' arrival at Yerba Buena doubled the size of the
village, but had no immediate impact on Sutter's Fort.

Brannan himself, a shrewd man whose agile mind hummed with
many private ambitions, would contribute to the downfall of John
Sutter's domain within two years.

FALL, 1846: OVERLAND IMMIGRATION

In the fall of 1846, an estimated 1,500 individuals streamed down over the Sierra Nevada into the Sacramento Valley, the largest influx of overland immigrants before the Gold Rush years. Many of the incoming men signed up for duty in the Mexican-American War before they even unhitched their wagons at Sutter's Fort. When the war ended, several came back to the Fort to work there, or establish farms in the vicinity. More of them, though, moved on with their families to Santa Clara Valley, Napa Valley, San Francisco, and other settlements.

Among those who settled in or near the Fort were Heinrich Lienhard and his trail companion George Zins; George McKinstry Junior, Peter Wimmer, and Samuel Kyburz. All of these men, led by Lansford Hastings, traversed the Great Salt Desert on the Hastings' Cutoff, ahead of the Donner Party.

Lienhard, George Zins, and George McKinstry were single. Zins, a French-born German who had the knack of being able to fix almost anything, "made himself useful" at the Fort after his discharge at Los Angeles in early 1847. In June 1847 he married Donner Party survivor Dorothea Wolfinger and moved southwest of the Fort to Sutterville, where he and his wife established the first kiln-fired-brick manufacturing business in the Sacramento Valley. George McKinstry, who did not participate in the war because of illness, accepted Sutter's appointment as the first sheriff in the Sacramento District, a post he held 1846-1847. As sheriff, McKinstry was involved in the rescue of the Donner Party, chiefly by writing letters to San Francisco newspapers in an effort to raise funds. McKinstry also functioned as Sutter's clerk and "advisor" for a time. He owned property in Sutterville and later was active in Sacramento civic affairs until 1851, when he moved to San Diego County.

Heinrich Lienhard, a twenty-four-year-old Swiss, worked in a variety of positions. He spent some months as overseer at Sutter's Hock Farm, and later worked as a gardener at Sutter's Fort. His most important job was as the supervisor and "keeper of the keys" at the

Fort, starting in September 1847 (when Samuel Kyburz relinquished the keys) until May 1848, when the Indian Olimpio became Key Keeper. In 1849, Lienhard was chosen to escort Sutter's wife and children from Switzerland to California.

After delivering the Sutter family to San Francisco in 1850, Lienhard returned to Switzerland, and married. In 1854 he moved back to the United States with his wife, settling in Wisconsin where he raised a large family.

Peter Wimmer, thirty-six in 1846, and Samuel Kyburz, also aged thirty-six, were married men.

Peter and Jenny Wimmer entered California with the combined seven children from their respective widowed first marriages, and later had four more children together. Wimmer, an experienced frontiersman with a working knowledge of Indian languages, was hired to accompany James Marshall in August 1847, when Marshall went to Coloma to build a sawmill for John Sutter. Sutter also hired Jenny Wimmer as the sawmill crew's cook and laundress. The Wimmers, and their children, were present at Coloma on the day Marshall discovered gold. In subsequent years they lived in various California locales, finally settling in San Diego County.

Samuel Kyburz, born in Oberentfelden, Aargau, Switzerland, emigrated to the United States in September 1833, with his father and brothers. He married Rebecca Sophia Barber in Spring Prairie, Wisconsin, in May 1841. In April 1846 Sam, Rebecca, their four-year-old son Samuel Elliott and two-year-old daughter Sarah, joined a large west-bound caravan at Independence, Missouri. They arrived at Sutter's Fort about mid-September.

Recognizing Samuel's managerial skills and reliability, Sutter hired him as the Fort's majordomo (superintendent). Kyburz supervised the employees who worked the wheat fields and livestock herds, was responsible for overseeing shipments going down the Sacramento River to San Francisco Bay, and performed a dozen other tasks.

Rebecca gave birth to a third child on February 9, 1848, at the Fort. The couple named the baby John Augustus Kyburz. Although he relinquished the Fort's keys and certain responsibilities to Heinrich Lienhard, probably because his other duties took him away from the Fort for extended periods, nothing else suggests that Samuel Kyburz stepped down from a managerial position until May 22, 1848. On that day Sutter entered in the logbook, "Mr. Kyburz left my services and established a boarding house."

Kyburz and his wife had decided to open a boarding house inside the Fort, because by May 1848 increasing numbers of would-be prospectors were swarming past on their way to the gold fields. Before the end of the year, though, the family moved to San Francisco, where the baby boy John Augustus died January 23, 1849, and another daughter was born later that month. Sam Kyburz and family lived at Sutter's Hock Farm during 1851-52, then in Sacramento for ten years. Afterward they resided in White Rock, El Dorado County, where Sam managed a roadhouse. Later, Kyburz and his sons owned a dairy business on 160 acres in Clarksburg. Samuel Kyburz died in 1898, in the home of his eldest son, at Shingle Springs.

The Kyburz Annex at Sutter's Fort did not exist in pioneer days but was added as a feature during the Fort's restoration in the 1890s.

The Central Building, once known as the Sutter House, seen from the west yard. *Photo by author.*

1846-1847:
PEACE, AND THE DONNER PARTY

On January 13, 1847, the Californians surrendered at Campo de Cahuenga in today's North Hollywood. The Treaty of Cahuenga was not a formal treaty between warring nations, but an informal agreement between rival military forces that ended the Mexican-American War only in California. Major Pierson B. Reading, the Fort's erstwhile head trapper, was one of five signatories to the mutually agreed-upon Articles of Capitulation.

This happy news may or may not have reached Sutter's Fort when a living skeleton, supported by two Indians, stumbled into the outskirts of William Johnson's ranch on the Bear River on January 17. His name was William Eddy. For thirty-two days, lost in blizzards and deep snow, he had struggled on to find help for his family and friends who were stranded at a small alpine lake, starving and trying to survive the intense cold in miserable hovels. Eddy and fourteen others had set out from that lake in desperation, on snow shoes. Only seven of them were still alive.

The rescue of the Donner Party is one of the most famous episodes in the history of Sutter's Fort. This wagon company's story of heroism, villainy, and cannibalism remains the most sensational and haunting tale in the annals of western migration.

It wasn't that no one knew they were still out there. The previous September, soon after the Donner Party entered eastern Nevada, members Charles Stanton and William McCutchen had ridden ahead to the Fort for provisions. McCutchen was too ill for a return trip, so Captain Sutter sent Stanton back with seven food-laden pack mules, plus two Indian cowherds to help Stanton manage the animals and guide him back to the wagons. James Reed, having been banished from the company for killing a teamster along the Humboldt River in the midst of a fiery argument turned deadly, turned up at the Fort on October 28.

But by then the first snow storms—early that year—were already blanketing a formidable mountain range notorious for some of the worst winter conditions on the continent. It was too dangerous now to attempt a crossing, either coming down or going up. Sutter's optimistic estimate, based on Reed's stale information, was that there was enough food, if they were careful, to sustain the party until spring. Nonetheless, Reed and a recovered McCutchen, supplied with more provisions by Sutter, decided to launch a rescue effort on their own. They left the Fort on October 31, but the deep snow forced them back well short of the mountain's crest.

Meanwhile, the Donner Party had reached the lake. Despite efforts to cross the pass, the party now numbering eighty-one men, women and children (counting Sutter's Indian *vaqueros* and the returned, selfless Stanton) admitted they were trapped about the same time that Reed and McCutchen were also admitting defeat. Unbeknownst to anyone in the Sacramento Valley, those earlier provisions from Sutter were all but depleted. Indians had killed many of the party's cattle in the Nevada desert, and the remaining cattle were soon buried beyond reach in deep snow drifts. Their situation was dire.

When William Eddy materialized at Johnson's in mid-January, a runner took the horrific news to the Sacramento District's magistrate, Sutter's neighbor John Sinclair. Mr. Sinclair was temporarily away, so Mrs. Sinclair notified the Fort's commander Edward Kern. Kern called for rescue party volunteers, promising the princely rate of three dollars per day to be paid by the government. When Sinclair returned, both he and John Sutter guaranteed that amount out of their own pockets should Kern's superiors not approve of the cost. Sutter sent his launch downriver to enlist the help of coastal residents, while he and Sinclair mustered mules and supplies and men—the last more problematic because most of the able-bodied young men had not yet returned from Los Angeles and San Diego, where most of the action of the Mexican-American War had taken place.

Fortunately, a few had not gone to war. The first of three brave groups of volunteers, risking their own lives, departed from Johnson's Ranch on February 5 and reached the lake encampments on February 19, 1847. The rescuers, known as Relief Parties, went on foot carrying heavy packs. So, too, the debilitated refugees had to walk out, as far as the waystation at Mule Springs—several days' journey—because horses and mules floundered and sank in the ten-to-thirty-foot snowdrifts beyond that point. Six refugees died while they were being led to safety.

Altogether, slightly more than half of the Donner Party survived. The rest perished from starvation and prolonged exposure to below-freezing temperatures. Only two families survived intact: James Reed, his wife Margret and their four children aged thirteen and under; and Patrick Breen, his wife Peggy and their seven children ranging in age from one to fourteen.

Lieutenant Edward Kern was in charge at the Fort during the Donner Party rescue. His papers contain lists of the crews, their daily pay, and the clothing and tools they received. Rescuers were paid $3.00 per day; those carrying supplies or otherwise assisting, received $1.50 per day.

Quantities of foodstuffs, coffee, calico, flannel yardage, and thread and needles, were taken to Johnson's Ranch and the camp at Mule Springs, for consumption and use by the refugees. Miscellaneous clothing and equipment given to the relief workers included shirts, stockings, underwear, tin buckets, and small tools. An item amongst Kern's reports is Alcalde John Sinclair's note written on a scrap of green paper: "One coverlid (a contemporary term for a bed quilt too short to cover the pillows) left with Mr. Denton valued at $20.00." The First Relief gave it to John Denton when he grew too weak to continue walking. His body was found by the Second Relief, still wrapped in the quilt.

The survivors were brought to Sutter's Fort to convalesce. It was the only facility within a hundred miles with the resources to feed and shelter them until they were strong enough to start over.

Five female survivors married at the Fort during the spring and early summer of 1847. Orphaned teenagers Mary Murphy, Mary Ann Graves, and Elitha Donner married men who had aided rescue operations by supplying or transporting provisions. Mrs. Dorothea Wolfinger, whose husband was murdered for his supposed money by a Donner Party teamster and hastily buried somewhere in Nevada's desert sands, married George Zins. Harriet Murphy Pike, whose husband had died from an accidental gunshot near Truckee Meadows, wed handsome Michael Nye of the 1841 Bartleson-Bidwell Party.

Dolly

Throughout the entire ordeal James Reed's daughter, eight-year-old Patty Reed, kept a secret source of comfort hidden in her dress pocket. Tiny Dolly was a wooden doll house figurine, with prettily painted face and hair, and a lovely cloth gown. While adults of the

Donner Party clung to their sanity with prayers and diary entries, the frightened little girl found hope in Dolly's seemingly sympathetic face. Patty, whose given name was Martha Jane, married Frank Lewis in 1856 and lived to be a grandmother. She died in 1923, bequeathing her considerable collection of Donner memorabilia to Sutter's Fort, to be delivered by her estate in 1946 on the one hundred-year anniversary of the Donner Party tragedy.

Dolly is on display at Sutter's Fort, where thousands of visitors from all over the world see her every year, the icon of a winter nightmare.

Patty Reed's best friend, Dolly.
Courtesy Sutter's Fort.

THE BEST YEARS

A busy and prosperous Sutter's Fort sketched by Lt. Joseph Revere.
Courtesy Sutter's Fort.

In its heyday Sutter's Fort was a very busy place, a veritable little village of shops and bustling activity where dozens of people were always coming or going. Some came seeking jobs, others came bringing freight or livestock; a few stopped by to meet up with a friend.

Incoming travelers from the coast brought mail and months-old newspapers from trading ships, as well as newsy gossip. Outbound travelers took letters to settlements along their routes. When important communications required immediate dispatch but no sojourner had materialized, mounted couriers took to the trails. Sutter's several watercraft constantly plied the Sacramento River down to San Francisco Bay, filled with passengers and wheat or barrels of salted fish; and upriver to Hock Farm to load melons and tomatoes. One frequently used vessel was Sutter's whimsically-named launch *Lady Drinkwater.*

By 1845 the Fort was semi-famous in the United States and Europe, thanks to published reports by explorers Frémont and Wilkes, independent adventurers' letters to eastern newspapers, and John Sutter's own marketing efforts. Nonetheless, it was still a rough-and-tumble frontier outpost where life was lived mostly outdoors, and household amenities, such as adequate supplies of conventional tableware, were few.

The whole establishment was a sprawling complex, comprised of a walled trading post, several outbuildings, huge corrals, gardens, grain fields, fisheries, a tannery, and a hog ranch some four miles south of the compound. Cattle and sheep grazed on acres of pasturelands. A mudbrick building for Sutter's cowherds stood outside the south wall west of the main gate, retaining its name "the vaquero barracks" long after others consecutively occupied it.

Another, larger barracks-style building stood east of the Fort, in the block between K and L, and Twenty-eighth and Twenty-ninth Streets, where Sutter General Hospital is now. It was a one-story structure oriented east-west, about eighty feet long and forty feet wide. John Sutter laid the foundation for this building on October 13, 1845, and it somehow acquired the nickname "the penitentiary"—probably as a joke. Almost certainly, it was intended as temporary immigrant housing from inception, because Sutter believed that immigration would substantially increase, and there were few sleeping quarters inside the Fort. Masonry partitions divided this structure into perhaps fourteen apartments, with a central hallway running its length. Entrances were batten doors along the sides of the building, and a chimney was placed at the western end. Windows were no more than openings in the walls; the floor was merely hard packed earth.

Some of the Donner Party survivors were housed in this building, most notably teenaged Elitha and Leanna Donner and their very young half-sisters Georgia, Frances, and Eliza. In June 1847, not long after they and other immigrants living there had relocated, the partition walls were knocked down to convert the compartmentalized barracks into a large one-room granary.

Everywhere in the complex, endless chores filled daylight hours. These chores increased in number during seasonal activities such as sheep shearing, soap and candle-making, and the intensive tasks of planting, harvesting, and cleaning wheat. Ditch digging or repairing fallen ditches around grain fields, and cleaning the yard, were frequent routines.

The roof of the beehive-shaped *horno* collapsed in October 1845 and had to be rebuilt. The following day, stone-cutter William Moon arrived from present-day Tehama County with new grindstones for the gristmill. A month later it too, broke, and had to be repaired. Work crews sank a new well in December, and hung new doors on shops. Men took whipsaws and froes to the "piney woods" to make beams, boards, shingles, and barrel staves.

Immigrants and their children died and were buried in the Fort's graveyard, now the site of Sutter Middle School at Alhambra and J streets. Now and then a doctor was in residence. The doctor who stayed the longest was Henry Bates, hired during the 1846 measles epidemic that decimated many of Sutter's Indian workers. Dr. Bates lived in the old vaquero barracks for a time.

Time for socializing was limited, which made Sarah (Mrs. Allen) Montgomery's quilting party on January 29, 1846—the first such event held in the Sacramento Valley—all the more enjoyable. All the neighbors went, even Captain Sutter's single male employees. Sarah's party was held in her own home. As more settlers arrived, the Fort became a natural place for far-apart farm families to gather and socialize on Sundays.

In hopes that more immigrants would settle in the Sacramento Valley, Sutter and his associates took time in 1846 to survey and plot a new town of two hundred lots, called Sutterville, on a rise of land approximately where Land Park is today. A few homes and shops were established there, and initially the town flourished. Ultimately, however, Sutterville was overshadowed by its bustling rival Sacramento City, and faded into obscurity after the mid-1850s.

The 1845 and 1846 immigrations had swelled the populace around the Fort, so 1847 was busier than ever. The blanket factory acquired more weavers. A larger *horno* to accommodate increased baking needs was built in June (although its roof fell in a week later). The tanning vats were given needed repairs. The chimney in the former immigrant barracks was dismantled to provide bricks for a new fire pit in the blacksmith shop. A tedious chore called "making oakum" occupied several hands for an entire day. The task involved unraveling and picking apart, thread by thread, old ropes and cordage into handfuls of loose fiber (oakum), which was used as a first step in packing and sealing cast iron pipe joints.

Incoming settlers purchased Sutter's manufactured wares, from hats or wooden barrels to shoes and leather bridles. They brought their wagons and equipment to the blacksmith for repairs, and transported their own wheat harvests to the Fort's gristmill.

Tools, hoops and barrels in the re-created cooper's shop. *Photo by author.*

The mill was inoperative for a few days in September 1847 while new grindstones and a new spindle were installed, and out of order entirely for a few days in October. When former Fort employee Jared Sheldon opened the second gristmill in the valley at his ranch on the Cosumnes River, wagonloads of grain from Sutter's Fort were sent there to be ground into flour because, although it was kept running day and night after the October repairs, the Fort's little horse-mill was rapidly becoming inadequate to meet increased demand.

Edward Kern was relieved of his command in late May 1847 by Lieutenant Charles Anderson, leading Company C of General Jonathan Stevenson's regiment of New York Volunteers.

The garrison moved into the Fort on June 1. Amiable and more experienced than artist-turned-soldier Kern, Anderson allowed Sutter to re-establish his position of authority on his own estate. In August, members of the discharged Mormon Battalion reached Sutter's Fort, headed east toward their homes in Utah. Several were experienced craftsmen who wanted jobs to tide them over for the coming winter before crossing the Sierra in the spring. Lieutenant Anderson's garrison pulled out on September 20, following his sudden death in San Francisco the previous week. This garrison was not replaced, possibly because word had already filtered back from the battlefront that Mexico City had fallen on September 14, unofficially ending the Mexican-American War.

On September 15, 1847, the logbook records—for the first time—that Sutter's employees, possibly the new men hired from among the recently-arrived Mormons, were busy plastering and whitewashing the Fort.

Peace and prosperity seemed close at hand. This state of affairs no doubt prompted the ambitious to consider their probable success if they opened a business at the only trading post in the interior—a trading post at the crossroads of established routes in all directions.

As early as May 1847, Honolulu-San Francisco merchant Samuel Norris had established a store in a mudbrick cabin near the tan yard. In September, James Coates, a tanner at the Fort since his arrival from Oregon in 1843, moved into a sheepherder's hut on the American River about two miles east of the Fort, and opened a second store. On October 12, C. C. Smith & Company opened a mercantile and *cantina* in the former vaquero barracks outside the Fort's south wall. Charles C. Smith ran the business; the "and Company" was his partner Samuel Brannan, the Mormon Elder who had brought a shipload of the faithful to California in July 1846. All three stores were paying rent.

John Sutter decided to move forward with projects that had been on hold for many long months.

Definitely, the time was long overdue to replace the little horse-mill with a larger, water-powered gristmill. Too, Sutter wanted a sawmill to provide board lumber for Fort improvements, and to sell to incoming settlers. The discharged Mormon soldiers, who added up to a sizeable infusion of skilled workers, were hardly off their horses before he hired several to build a new gristmill on the American River, about six miles east of the Fort. On August 27, 1847, he signed a partnership agreement with his chief handyman James Marshall to construct a sawmill in a little foothills valley called Coloma, forty-odd miles distant. For this project, the new partners hired a smaller crew of six Mormons, augmented by three more Fort employees of longer standing. Arriving at the chosen site, the crew's first priority was to build cabins for shelter. Work on the sawmill commenced around the end of September.

On December 25, 1847, the tanners and shoemakers hosted a Christmas dinner in the hatter's shop for all of the Fort's employees. It was the last party of its kind for many years to come.

The Fort's best years are generally considered to be 1845–1847—just before a startling discovery in the very ground the longed-for sawmill stood on wrecked havoc upon it.

GOLD! AND RUIN

On January 24, 1848, James Marshall was inspecting the sawmill's tailrace when he noticed something shiny at the bottom… and by leaning down to pick it up, changed the course of history.

News of Marshall's gold discovery at Coloma flashed around the world—but not immediately. During February and March, activities at the Fort hummed along as usual, despite intermittent heavy rains. Laborers sowed wheat and peas, worked on the coal pit, drove wagons with provisions to the two new mill sites, tended a delivery of livestock, and so

Sutter's sawmill at Coloma, where gold was discovered. *Courtesy Library of Congress.*

forth. Rumors had started to spread, though, despite the mill crew's promises to keep quiet about the gold discovery. April brought sheep shearing season and a slight increase in the number of curious locals who stopped in or camped overnight outside the walls, en route to Coloma.

On May 12, 1848—after he had quietly stocked his stores with every pan, pick and shovel he could find—Sam Brannan rode through the streets of San Francisco waving a bottle of gold dust and shouting, "Gold! Gold on the American River!" His action launched a stampede to the gold fields, the genesis of his own immense wealth, and the beginning of the end of John Sutter's dreams of empire.

Coincidentally, on the same day Brannan was parading through San Francisco, the Fort was given an overall coat of whitewash. Two days later, the former immigrant barracks-cum-granary was cleaned out, whitewashed, and rented to C. C. Smith & Company for a store.

The following week Smith moved in, vacating his original store premises in the old vaquero barracks so that Samuel Kyburz, the Fort's superintendent since 1846, could use it to establish a boarding house. Kyburz, however, decided that the second floor of the Central Building was more suited to his purpose. Instead Samuel Norris, who already operated a store near the tan yard, moved into the vaquero barracks, hanging a sign on the front that read, "Retail Store S. Norris." Sam Brannan bought out Charles C. Smith, acquired wealthier and more socially prominent men as partners, and reorganized as S. Brannan & Co.

May ended. Disorder and confusion descended on the Fort as almost all of Sutter's workmen deserted for the gold-filled foothills.

Escalating Gold Frenzy

James Coates, Brannan and Norris weren't the only merchants, nor Kyburz the only service provider. When California's military governor Colonel Richard Barnes Mason visited the Fort in early July, he was a bit stunned to find so much frenetic activity: launches discharging their cargoes at the river, carts hauling goods to and fro, men scurrying everywhere, and prices skyrocketing. His official report to his superiors noted that Brannan's store had sold $36,000 in goods from the first of May to the tenth of July, and that other merchants had also made extensive sales. Brannan, and several others, sold shirts, tents, linens, blankets, jackets, saddles, hats, foodstuffs, and mining equipment. Shoes were at a premium. Early on, ordinary shoes that sold for seventy-five cents per pair in Boston cost $8 to $12 in California. In a short time prices in California "standardized," based on the going rate for gold at $16 per ounce.

Deserting workers meant vacant workshops at the Fort, spaces quickly filled by yet more mercantile outlets, two saloons, and a billiard parlor. The bottom floor of the Central Building housed a gambling den that served liquor. Once the desired goal of trail-worn wagon trains, Sutter's Fort was now, instead, a rendezvous for prospectors going to or coming from the mines. Said Heinrich Lienhard, "Within a short time the fort... became the center of every kind of vice; gambling, cheating, robbing, drinking, and even murder were daily events and few traces of law and order remained."

Lienhard, the young Swiss who had been the Fort's supervisor until May 1848, abhorred drinking and gambling and therefore harbored a strong dislike of the gold-frenzied men who were far removed from the constraints of their homes. This statement in his memoir written many years after the events reflects those views, although he may have exaggerated a bit. No other contemporary claimed that murder was a daily event at Sutter's Fort.

Nevertheless, the noise, carousing, and general wanton behavior *was* offensive, and frightening, to others as well. Samuel and Rebecca Kyburz, who had two small children and an infant, moved to San Francisco, probably in the late summer or fall of 1848. Rufus Hitchcock moved in with his adult son and two daughters to run the boardinghouse. Despite complaints about the quality of food they served, the Hitchcocks lasted until the spring of 1849 because Rufus also operated the gambling den.

Two ordinary services were still offered. Ephraim Fairchild, who had entered Sutter's service in 1847 as a wagon maker (a sideline craft practiced by many blacksmiths) remained as the Fort's blacksmith and gunsmith. Like everyone else, he charged exorbitant rates: $16 (an ounce of gold) for the smallest repair job on gun or pistol; $16 for shoeing one foot of a horse or mule, and $64 for all four hooves. Fairchild had an assistant to work his forge's bellows, whom he paid $16 per day.

During the winter of 1848-1849 a tinsmith named Joseph Wadleigh appeared with a set of tools and a supply of tin plate. Erecting a shanty for himself between Brannan's store and the Fort, Wadleigh was soon engaged in the manufacture of large pans—which were as indispensible to the miners as picks or shovels—and readily sold them for $16 apiece. He accumulated a fortune before the summer of 1849.

Meanwhile, in September 1848, Captain Sutter's son John Augustus Sutter Junior, familiarly known as August, arrived at the Fort where he quickly discovered the extent of his father's debts. From the day he had landed back in 1839, John Sutter Senior had needed more commodities than he could afford just to keep his little colony afloat: more supplies, more materials, more tools and equipment. To acquire these things, he had made complex, imprudent promises to various suppliers. Worst of all, he still owed the Russians a substantial portion of the Fort Ross purchase price. His financial condition was a muddled, disastrous morass. But now, erroneously assuming that Sutter was suddenly wealthy, creditors were clamoring for payment—in particular the Russians, who were threatening to foreclose on their mortgage.

Thinking to stall his creditors and keep his holdings safe, Sutter Senior transferred title to his son on October 14, and soon thereafter departed for the gold mines to try his own luck. August, just turned twenty-two, was a conscientious, though naïve, young man who wanted to save as much as possible of his father's property before it might be lost to the Sutter family forever. But this transfer of ownership gave August the right to convey any property within the New Helvetia grant, and August was no match for men who were far craftier than he.

Boat loads of gold-seekers were already landing at the *embarcadero*. The merchants who sold mining implements and supplies wanted to build a town on the riverfront, so they convinced August that the sale of town lots would provide funds to pay off his father's debts. In December August hired Captain William Warner, on leave from the Army Topographical Corps, to survey and map a new town. In January 1849, lots for the new city of Sacramento went on the auction block and sold briskly. Sam Brannan purchased Lot 1 in block K-L-28-29 (the corner of Twenty-eighth and K Streets), the land beneath Sutter's immigrant barracks/granary, which now housed Brannan's store.

And while those town lots were still being surveyed and mapped in December, August began selling the Fort—piecemeal—thus instigating a complicated chain of ownership that spanned nearly forty years.

JAMES MARSHALL

James Wilson Marshall.
Courtesy Sutter's Fort.

Born October 8, 1810, James Wilson Marshall was the son of carpenter and wheelwright Philip Marshall, and his wife Sarah. The family lived in New Jersey, where James and his sisters attended school. James did well in the sciences, learned his father's trade, and developed into a skilled woodworker and mechanic. At age fifteen, after a heated quarrel with his father, he ran away from home.

Marshall wandered about the Atlantic Coast, working mostly at sawmills and lumber companies. During the 1830s he settled in Missouri, where he bought a farm. After a bout with malaria, he sold the farm in 1844 and joined a wagon train headed to Oregon where the air was supposedly healthier—but he thought winters in Oregon were too wet. The next year he went south, accepting employment at Sutter's Fort.

To John Sutter, Marshall was a godsend: a man who could build or repair almost anything. At Sutter's establishment he made spinning wheels and looms, carts and wagons, built beds and tables, and rigged up frontier-style machinery. In June 1846 Marshall accompanied Lt. John Frémont to reinforce the Bear Flaggers at Sonoma, then joined Frémont's volunteers to fight in the Mexican-American War. When the war ended and Marshall returned to the Fort in 1847, he was the logical choice to build the lumber mill Sutter had long wanted.

The mill Marshall designed was a simple construct, of a type he had seen many times. The work was nearing completion except for the tailrace, a ditch which was initially too shallow to carry water fast enough past the wheel that powered the saw. The crew dug it deeper, and then let water pour through it overnight to scour the bottom. The flowing water trapped particles of gold from the loosened gravel banks into the cracks of the exposed bedrock... the shining flakes Marshall saw when he inspected the deepened channel the next morning. He wasn't sure it was gold at first.

Most people who knew Marshall thought he was strange. He was moody, eccentric, and often surly. He had mystical visions. After the sawmill was completed in March 1848 Marshall couldn't find competent help to operate it, so he turned to prospecting but never made a big strike. Nevertheless, fortune seekers dogged his every move, certain he would lead them to the proverbial pot of gold. When he couldn't, they got angry. Finally, he was forced to sell his interest in the sawmill just to buy food.

After failing at a number of ventures over the years, an embittered Marshall spent his last days eking out a living as a blacksmith in Kelsey, a few miles from Coloma. He died there on August 10, 1885. His friends had to auction off his meager belongings just to cover his funeral expenses.

James Marshall was not the first person to find gold in California, but it was his discovery that launched the California Gold Rush.

SAM BRANNAN

Samuel Brannan is credited with being California's first millionaire. A printer by trade, he was a tycoon at heart, loading a printing press and complete flour mill equipment aboard the *Brooklyn* when the ship sailed from New York in February 1846. In January 1847, Brannan founded San Francisco's first newspaper, the *California Star*. By year's end he owned a hotel, a flour mill, and a store.

Samuel Brannan. *Author's collection.*

By mid-1848 he owned several stores, his first one in San Francisco and others at Sutter's Fort, Coloma, and Sutterville. In early 1849 he opened yet another in fledgling Sacramento City. He built the City Hotel there, using lumber from Sutter's abandoned gristmill on the American River. Always an opportunist, Sam quickly acquired about one-fourth of the lots in Sacramento, as well as one-fifth of the lots in San Francisco. In fact, he owned land all over northern California, including areas that became Yuba and Sutter Counties. Elected to San Francisco's town council, he was an influential force in organizing San Francisco's first Vigilance Committee in 1851. His boat, the *Dice Mi Nana*, hauled profitable merchandise over the Sacramento and San Joaquin Rivers. In 1859 he developed the resort town of Calistoga.

Born March 2, 1819, in Saco, Maine, Sam left home at age fourteen to live with his sister and brother-in-law in Painesville, Ohio. There, he apprenticed as a printer, and in 1842 joined the Church of Jesus Christ of Latter Day Saints. Excommunicated twice by Brigham Young, and divorced twice, it was Brannan's second bitter and very costly divorce in 1870 that brought down his shaky real estate empire, much of which was founded on credit. His womanizing ways and indulgence in drink caught up with him, too. Brannan tried to recoup his fortune through various real estate schemes in California and Mexico that never quite panned out. He died a near-pauper on May 5, 1889, in Escondido.

SELLING THE FORT

On December 20, 1848, Alden Bayley and his partner Michael McClellan purchased, for $2,000, the rights to use the Central Building as a hotel, which ultimately made them the landlords of Rufus Hitchcock, the man who operated the gambling den on the ground floor. Both had migrated to California in the 1848 overland travel season, originally headed for Oregon with their families until they learned of the gold discovery while still east of the Sierra. In March 1849, August Sutter sold them this building outright, plus certain adjacent areas within a 160-foot square space surrounding the structure, for $7,000.

The Central Building became known as the Sutter House.

On December 28, 1848, August sold a substantial section along the south wall to merchants Hensley, Reading & Co. for $6,500. Their boundary began east of the main gate (the south gate, facing L Street), and continued eastward around the corner to encompass the southeast bastion and a short section along the east wall. Within six months, though, Hensley, Reading & Co. pieced out their holdings to other businessmen. One transaction was the lease of a significant portion of their space along the south wall to Peter Slater, who installed a bowling alley.

Also on December 28, August sold two rooms north of the east gate, the northeast corner, and another adjacent room along the north wall to Dr. Victor Fourgeaud, a San Francisco physician who never occupied the premises and probably bought only as an investment, for $1,700. Ten months later, Dr. Fourgeaud sold his rooms at a loss to Charles E. Pickett, who personally operated a general store.

On December 30, 1848, August sold a large portion on the north side, east of the Central Building, to merchants Priest, Lee and Company for $3,500. The eastern end of their property abutted Dr. Fourgeaud's suite of rooms, then extended west along the north wall to the corral on the west side of the Central Building.

In May 1849, Hensley, Reading & Co. sold the southeast bastion to Dr. W. Grove Deal, for $4,000, which he used as a hospital until

December, when doctors James S. Martin and Benjamin R. Carman took over his practice. The Fort's southeast bastion, originally larger than it is today, served as the main hospital in Sacramento through the cholera epidemic in 1850.

The blacksmith Ephraim Fairchild purchased his southwest corner—two rooms on the south wall and two along the southwest wall—for $2,600 on November 6, 1849.

The distillery and kitchen buildings were stand-alone structures in Sutter's time. The distillery building and adjacent land was sold to Lewis J. Sagat and Charles C. Southard on March 1, 1849. Their property began at the west side of the small north gate and went all the way west to include the gristmill around the corner from the northwest bastion. They stayed in business at the Fort through August 1849. Sagat and Southard sold general mining supplies; they were not interested in either producing or storing alcohol. August Sutter removed the working still from the premises and sold it to Mariano Vallejo in April 1849, for $400.

The earlier sale to Bayley and McClellan included the kitchen, which sat inside the 160-foot square boundary that surrounded the Central Building, the three connected rooms Sutter had constructed upon his arrival in 1839, and the corral directly east of those rooms. Alden Bayley either regretted his purchase, or wanted funds with which to buy another property, because a few days after he bought his interest in the Sutter House from August Sutter, he resold it to Richard D. Torney for $10,000. Within a year Torney defaulted, and Bayley reclaimed the property.

Bayley's partner soon wanted out, too. In August 1849, Michael McClellan placed this advertisement:

For Sale!
The Subscriber having determined to return to the United States with his family, offers for sale the following property, viz: his undivided half of the large and commodious adobe hotel, situated in Fort Sutter in Sacramento City and known as the Sutter House, together with the corral and outbuildings, consisting of a large bake house and rooms adjoining, suitable for dwelling houses; also a good well with patent pump, etc. This is the best public house property in the Sacramento Valley, and has all the fixtures necessary for carrying on an extensive

and lucrative business; and cannot fail to make a fortune for any person who will purchase it and conduct it property.

Either no one offered to buy, or wouldn't meet his terms. The McClellan family stayed on at the Fort for a while even after McClellan lost his undivided one-half interest to Bayley in a November 1850 court action.

Not all of the first-tier owners or renters are included in the transactions cited above. From this beginning, though, the parade of owners grows ever more complex as original buyers moved out and sold to others—who resold to still others—creating a maze of land titles, defaults, and several disputes over ownership. In 1869, John Garland purchased the entire grounds, whereupon he proceeded to fence the Fort property and surrounding blocks. Arrested for blocking the streets, Garland was forced to sell. His buyer was H. O. Beatty, who paid $12,000.

Finally, during 1871-1874, the Sutter's Fort property and certain of the surrounding blocks belonged to several large land owners. They did not live on the Fort grounds, but permitted a Mr. Corder to occupy the premises beginning in February 1873. Corder used the

A storage room inside a north wall shed. *Photo by author.*

site for the business of soap making, and the production of chickens by means of artificial incubation.

The last sole owner was Benjamin Merrill, a real estate mogul who lived in Chicago. Merrill rented out the grounds for pastureland. There was nothing else left to rent, because the only structure still standing, albeit in a serious state of dilapidation, was the Central Building.

THE FORT'S FALL FROM GRACE

In the space of only eight years, John Sutter had transformed a raw wilderness into a large estate, and had achieved enviable prominence. As 1847 closed, he had reason to be hopeful that good times were coming—prosperous, peaceful years in which to pay off all his debts.

The gold discovery crushed those hopes. True, Sutter had declined an offer by the Mexican government in 1845 to purchase his land grant, and he had offered to sell the Fort to the United States in 1846, during the Mexican-American War. Those options, had they come to anything, would have given him substantial cash and allowed a graceful retreat. Now, overwhelmed by gold miners who butchered his cattle and trampled his wheat fields, and "friends" who defrauded him left and right, a bewildered and embittered Sutter removed to his Hock Farm on the Feather River. Once he was gone, no one cared about his magnificent structure.

The Fort's new owners knocked large holes through the walls to accommodate new doors and windows, and removed partitions. Someone stole the forged bell from the west yard. A few vendors literally took the bricks, joists, and beams of their shops with them when they moved on to Sacramento. Newcomers to the city removed mud bricks from the outer walls, and eventually the gates and roof shingles, for building materials. When Margaret Frink's covered wagon rolled past the Fort in September 1850, she noted that it was "deserted and going to decay," but Mrs. Frink didn't realize that people were still living there or that there was other activity inside.

In 1850 the Richard Torney and Michael McClellan families were still in residence, and a hospital jointly operated by the Masons and Odd Fellows occupied the southeast bastion. In August 1849, Sam Brannan had closed his store near the Fort in favor of another building he had erected on Front Street in the blossoming new city, and sold the lot at Twenty-eighth and K. Thus, the Fort's old immigrant barracks-turned-mercantile shop next became Sacramento Hospital. The first doctor to practice there, Charles Cragin, advertised in both San Francisco's *Weekly Alta California* and the *Placer Times* that the "commodious building" had been thoroughly refitted and re-furnished.

The *Placer Times*, Sacramento's first newspaper, began its life on the Fort's grounds, publishing its first issue on April 28, 1849, from a cloth-ceilinged shanty near Brannan's store. In July, the newspaper moved to new offices in the city.

And so it went. By 1851 the merchants were all gone. Pillage escalated, and by 1853 only the Sutter House (the Central Building), the southeast bastion, sections of the outer walls, and some of the shop buildings remained. Meantime, in 1850 a bridge had been built over the slough for the benefit of Sacramento merchants and teamsters who daily transported goods to the upland mines. In January 1853, the *Sacramento Daily Union* announced that the slough had been re-bridged after heavy rain storms in the winter of 1852 had destroyed the original.

In April 1852 Alden Bayley, who now owned all of the Central Building and adjacent grounds despite his active efforts to unload it, offered to sell what he termed "the larger part of the facility" to the State of California, for $5,000. Recommending that it be used as a lunatic hospital, Bayley cited the attic and ground floor, nine furnished rooms on the second floor, a large bake house, three storerooms in the rear of the building, two water wells, and a corral. Bayley further assured his prospective buyer that the furnished rooms on the second floor were fit for immediate use, and that "a very small outlay" would "adapt the whole to the purpose proposed." The legislature took no action on Bayley's offer.

Some eighteen months later, Bayley evidently gave up hope and put up the Sutter House for sale at public auction. In a bizarre twist of fate, Olive Torney—widow of the same Richard Torney who had defaulted on his $10,000 purchase of the Sutter House from Bayley back in 1850—bought it for $451 on January 26, 1854. She and her children had been living in the building for some years, presumably renting. In October 1854 Olive Torney married Norman

Lawson, who formed a headquarters at the Fort for his company of game hunters.

About 1857, the roof and interior floors of the Fort's southeast bastion caved in. Undaunted, Olive Torney Lawson and her children cleaned up some of the rubble and carried on. In September 1860 Mrs. Lawson filed a Declaration of Homestead for the section of Sutter's Fort she was living in, stating that her home was "known as the Sutter House, said premises situated on a lot or parcel of ground about 160 feet square."

The southeast bastion circa 1855, with collapsed interior floors. *Courtesy Sutter's Fort.*

Then came the 1861-62 so-called Monster Storms—week after week of unrelenting rain that caused severe flooding throughout California and three adjacent states—turning the Sacramento and San Joaquin valleys into lakes. Thousands were suddenly without food or shelter as Sacramento residents scrambled to their rooftops or the top floors of hotels.

Sacramento's Howard Benevolence Society sprang into action, coordinating rescue efforts and donations from San Francisco of food, bedding, clothing, and boats for transportation. The Society established eight emergency stations to receive and aid the needy. One of the eight stations was at the Agricultural Society's multi-storied Pavilion at Sixth and M Streets, and another was on the high ground of Sutter's Fort. This was the last station to be closed, and Mrs. Olive Lawson, who had charge of that station, was commended in print for her "excellent management and care... in relieving the large number of people under her protection."

The Fort was not inundated during this catastrophic event; but the storms undercut the ground beneath the north wall, causing it to collapse.

Olive Lawson and family continued to live in the Sutter House until 1868, when one of several owner-investors in the K-L-26-28 streets city blocks was successful in evicting them. A year later all remaining title holders conveyed their properties to John Garland. This action began the chain of ownership that culminated in Benjamin Merrill's purchase of the Fort in 1874, as previously noted.

By this time the south wall of the Central Building was showing signs of disintegration and its outside wooden stairs were rotting. Abandoned and decaying, the former Sutter House stood on its knoll and waited.

The once-vital Central Building, in ruins. *Courtesy Sutter's Fort.*

THE CLERKS AT SUTTER'S FORT

In the early nineteenth century, clerks were not entry-level employees. In an era when only about 60 per cent of the population was literate, clerks were educated men who were hired as middle-management. These are the men who held that position at the Fort.

Octave (Octavio) Custot was the first clerk and overseer at Sutter's Fort, 1839-early 1840s. A French fur trapper educated in his native country, Custot arrived in California in 1837. The following year he worked for Mariano Vallejo but was fired when Vallejo learned that Custot was stealing Peruvian sugar from his kitchens, and passing it off as newly-processed beet sugar. As a friend of Vicente Martinez (the son of Don Ignacio Martinez, from whom Sutter purchased his first cattle and other supplies), Custot had first-hand knowledge of Sutter's arrival and intentions to create a colony. He drifted into Sutter's employment in the fall of 1839.

Charles Flügge came to California in 1841 with the Bidwell-Bartleson Party. He was born in Germany, and had some legal training. From 1842-43 he was Sutter's chief clerk, business manager, confidant, and ambassador-at-large. Naturalized as a Mexican citizen in 1843, Flügge was granted a rancho on the Feather River; but after an acrimonious falling-out with Sutter, he moved to Los Angeles and opened a store.

After completing his fourteen-month assignment at Fort Ross, a stint as the overseer of Sutter's Hock Farm 1843-44, and one of Sutter's aides during the Micheltorena campaign, **John Bidwell** became Sutter's chief manager and bookkeeper in the spring of 1845. Bidwell exclusively wrote the daily entries in the *New Helvetia Diary* September 9, 1845, to September 27, 1845. From December 11, 1845, to December 9, 1846, he shared this duty with William N. Loker.

William Francis Swasey, co-leader of the Swasey-Todd Party, arrived at Sutter's Fort on September 23, 1845. He was only twenty-two, but because of the education he had acquired in his home state of Maine, Captain Sutter hired him as an assistant clerk to cover for John Bidwell, who was ill at the time. The entries in the *New Helvetia Diary* were exclusively written by Swasey from September 28 to October 25, 1845, and alternately by Swasey and Bidwell from October 25 to December 10, 1845. In January 1846, Swasey moved on. In Monterey, from June through September of 1846, he worked as a clerk for merchant and U.S. Consul to Mexican California Thomas O. Larkin. After the Mexican-American War, Swasey relocated to San Francisco, where he was elected the secretary of the town council. William Swasey died in San Francisco on Christmas Day, 1896.

William N. Loker of St. Louis arrived at Sutter's Fort on Christmas Day, 1845, as a member of Lansford Hastings' small entourage. He was a trader by occupation. Loker entered service as assistant clerk on Thursday, January 1, 1846, a job he kept through the late spring of 1846. He was the first Fort employee assigned to guard the Bear Flag prisoners, a task he hated. Loker enlisted in the California Battalion in June or July 1846 as a first lieutenant in Company A, which was chiefly composed of John Charles Frémont's original explorers. Later, he was assigned as an adjutant to Colonel Frémont. Loker was back at Sutter's Fort in June 1847, to announce the imminent arrival of Frémont's superior officer General Stephen Watts Kearny, with a defiant Frémont in tow. Loker accompanied his fallen hero overland to Washington, D.C. for Frémont's court martial, where he testified for the defense. He may be the same William N. Loker who arrived in San Francisco in March 1850, aboard the *Kingston*. In any case, in 1876 William Loker was known to be a broker in St. Louis.

After traversing the Hastings Cutoff ahead of the Donner Party, **George McKinstry Jr.** reached Sutter's Fort October 19, 1846. Because his poor health prevented him from participating in the Mexican-American War, George remained at the Fort, where he accepted Captain Sutter's appointments as his personal business manager and sheriff of the Sacramento District. In 1847, McKinstry became the overseer and chief clerk at Sutter's Fort. However, the Sutter-McKinstry relationship turned sour during the Sutterville vs. Sacramento City struggles for dominance in 1848-49. Born in Hudson, New York, probably in 1810, George was educated in New York and there, or later, acquired some knowledge of medicine. In late 1851 McKinstry moved to San Diego County, where he practiced medicine for several years from the home of John and Serafina Minter. When the Minters moved to Santa Ana George accompanied them, dying there about 1890.

THE BLACKSMITHS

O ver the years, several blacksmiths plied their trade at Sutter's Fort. These two were there the longest and are the best known.

John Chamberlain

One of the more colorful characters among the Fort's employees, John Chamberlain was somewhat of a ruffian, and an enthusiastic ladies' man. So enthusiastic, in fact, that his efforts to acquire female companionship were a constant source of irritation and bemusement to Captain Sutter. The historian Hubert Bancroft wrote, "Popular tradition has it that Chamberlain was "married" 19 times." These wives were Indian women, until he married immigrant Nancy Hess in January 1846.

A native of Ireland, Chamberlain left his homeland to go to sea on a whaling vessel, in 1839 jumping ship somewhere along the coast of Mexico. Making his way from Acapulco to California, he was working in Monterey as a blacksmith in 1840. He was arrested, along with many other foreigners, for his part in the so-called "Graham Affair."

This incident, which involved the deportation of transplanted Tennessean Isaac Graham and his fellow rowdies, led to a diplomatic crisis affecting Mexico, the United States, and the United Kingdom. Chamberlain was not imprisoned or exiled; instead, he was ordered to manufacture the shackles for the other prisoners. The following year Chamberlain worked for Monterey merchant Thomas O. Larkin, then in 1842 moved to Sutter's Fort where he was hired as a blacksmith.

Illness kept John Chamberlain from joining Sutter's troops in the Micheltorena campaign. He became a naturalized Mexican citizen in 1844, and received title to Rancho Socayac on the Cosumnes River. The ranch covered about 13,000 acres, but John's new father-in-law, John Henry Hess, was dead set on moving to Oregon. In March 1846 Chamberlain sold the ranch to Sutter's employee Perry McCoon and departed for Oregon with Nancy and her family. Eighteen years later he reappeared in Monterey, still a blacksmith, but with a different wife.

Samuel Neal

Samuel Neal arrived at Sutter's Fort in early March 1844, as a member of Lt. John Charles Frémont's Topographical Corps. Impressed with his skills, Fremont had hired him when the two met in Pennsylvania, where Neal had been a blacksmith for some years. The story is that twenty-seven-year-old Neal agreed to go with Frémont on the condition that he would have the option to leave the army explorer's outfit when they reached the Far West. True to his word, Frémont allowed Neal to accept employment with John Sutter, who was delighted to gain the services of an experienced blacksmith.

Neal was among Sutter's troops in January 1845, when Sutter and his makeshift army rode out on the ill-fated campaign to suppress a revolt against Governor Micheltorena. As a reward for his services, Neal was granted the 22,000-acre Rancho Esquon on the east side of Butte Creek. There, he realized his dream of breeding fine horses, a vocation he became famous for. Part of his investment in breeding stock, and other properties adjacent to his original land grant, came from striking it very rich during the Gold Rush. Reportedly, his Indian workers mined $110,000 in gold from Neal's claim on the Feather River.

It was Sam Neal who led Marine lieutenant Archibald Gillespie, bearing "secret government messages" to Frémont's camp at Klamath Lake in 1846, and Sam Neal who delivered Frémont's requisition for supplies to the USS *Portsmouth*, anchored in San Francisco Bay. A surgeon aboard the ship described Neal as "a very singular being... fearless as he can be. His costume is a white hat, ragged cloth jacket, tight breeches, buckskin leggings and shoes of the same material. His hair [had never seen a comb] and his face and hands are strangers to soap and water." Neal took part in the Bear Flag Revolt, but returned to Rancho Esquon to wait out the Mexican-American War. He died of pneumonia in 1859, aged forty-three. Most of his wealth in land and livestock was left to his family in the East, although Fanny, his daughter with an Indian wife, received a generous bequest, and a guardian to care for her.

NAMESAKE PLACES

Between 1839 and 1848, dozens of pioneers worked at Sutter's Fort, or lived nearby. Hundreds passed through on their way to settle elsewhere. John Sutter and many of the people he knew have their names enshrined on California maps and monuments. Here is a sampling.

Bidwell's Bar, Butte County
Established in July 1848 by John Bidwell at the site of his gold discovery on the Feather River, Bidwell's Bar was a thriving gold camp and major trading center from 1848 to 1856, and the seat of Butte County 1853-56. Today it is submerged beneath Lake Oroville. Monument #330 on Bidwell Canyon Road in the Oroville State Recreation Area marks the site as a California Historical Landmark. There is a Bidwell Street in Folsom, and another in San Francisco.

Brannan Island, Sacramento County
Brannan Island in the Sacramento Delta is named for flamboyant Sam Brannan, who founded his fortune—in part—with stores at Sutter's Fort before and after the gold discovery. Reclaimed from swampland in 1921, a significant portion of Brannan Island is now a state-owned park and recreation area. Streets, schools, watercourses, and other parks in California are also named for Sam Brannan.

Chiles Valley, Napa County, and Chiles Road, Yolo County
Joseph Ballinger Chiles first came to California with the Bidwell-Bartleson Party in 1841. Between 1842 and 1853 he made seven more cross-country trips, bringing new settlers each time. In 1844 he received the Rancho Catacula in Napa Valley as a Mexican land grant, and in 1850 purchased part of the Rancho Laguna de Santos Calle in Yolo County.

Donner Lake, Nevada County

Formerly known as Truckee Lake, the name was changed to honor the Donner Party, which was trapped here without adequate food or shelter during the winter of 1846-47. Almost half of them died from exposure and starvation. Survivors rescued in February-March 1847 were brought to Sutter's Fort to recuperate. Donner Memorial State Park wraps around the east, and part of the south shores, of Donner Lake. Landscape features Donner Pass, and Donner Peak, also commemorate this company's winter ordeal.

Folsom, Sacramento County

Originally named Granite City, this gold-mining town and railroad terminus changed its name to honor its founder, Captain Joseph L. Folsom, following his death in 1855. Captain Folsom was with Colonel Richard B. Mason when the colonel and his retinue were the honored guests at Sutter's Fort for the July 4, 1848 celebration. Upon William's Leidesdorff's death in 1848, Folsom purchased the Rancho Rio de los Americanos from Leidesdorff's mother.

Foster's Bar, Yuba County

This was a mining camp on the North Yuba River established in 1849 by William McFadden Foster, a Donner Party survivor who also participated in the rescue efforts. He was the husband of Sarah Ann Murphy Foster, son-in-law of Levinah Jackson Murphy (who perished); brother-in-law of Mary Murphy Johnson Covillaud. The Foster family moved to Minnesota in 1850, but Foster's Bar was a thriving township for decades. In 1970, the site was inundated by the Bullards Bar Reservoir.

Kelsey, El Dorado County and Kelseyville, Lake County

Benjamin Kelsey, a member of the 1841 Bartleson-Bidwell Party with his wife Nancy and their young daughter, staked out a rich claim eleven miles from Coloma in 1848. First known as Kelsey's Diggings, the place became a large camp within a year. During its heyday Kelsey boasted six hotels, twelve stores, and twenty-four saloons and gambling houses. A post office operated in Kelsey from 1859 to 1872; mining was conducted in the area until the 1960s. Kelseyville, located six miles southeast of Lakeport, is named for Benjamin's brother Andrew, also a member of the 1841 Bartleson-Bidwell Party, who purchased a ranch near Clear Lake in 1847 and died there in 1849.

Kern County, Kern River

Kern County derives its name from the Kern River. In 1845 explorer John Charles Frémont re-named the Rio San Felipe in honor of Edward Meyer Kern, who—the story goes—nearly drowned in its turbulent waters. Kern was Frémont's topographer and landscape artist on his third expedition through the American West. The following year, Frémont placed Edward Kern in command at Sutter's Fort, relegating Sutter to second place at his own establishment until Kern left the Fort in May 1847.

Knights Landing, Yolo County and Knights Ferry, Stanislaus County

Both communities were established by William Henry Knight, a former scout, fur trader and sometime-physician of sorts. He arrived in southern California in 1841 with the Workman-Rowland Party, overland from New Mexico via the Spanish Trail. In 1843 William, with his wife and children, settled on a tract of land along the Sacramento River where he founded Knights Landing. This location made him a "neighbor" of John Sutter's, and his name appears with some regularity in the Fort's logbook. Knight was persuaded to join the Bear Flag Revolt, but he refused to do more than act as a Spanish language interpreter. In the spring of 1849 the Knight family moved to a site on the Stanislaus River, where he established a trading post and a ferry. Knights Ferry became an important stage and supply center, but William didn't live to see the town's prosperity. He was cold-bloodedly murdered in the street on November 9, 1849, by a man whose name is lost to history.

Kyburz, El Dorado County

Located along the South Fork of the American River on the stage and wagon road to Carson Valley, this alpine community was originally named Slippery Ford. In the late 1850s Richard Yarnold, who owned the express service between Nevada and the Sacramento Valley, expanded an existing small cabin as a "hotel" and toll station. Twenty years later, a wealthy Californian rebuilt Yarnold's roadhouse strictly as a resort. In 1901 Albert B. Kyburz acquired the lodge, now a popular vacation destination he called Kyburz Station. The next year, Kyburz was appointed the Slippery Ford postmaster, a position which enabled him to have the name of the town officially changed to Kyburz. Albert did this not for himself, but to honor his late father Samuel A. Kyburz, the superintendent at Sutter's Fort 1846-48.

Lassen County and other Lassen namesakes

Born in 1800, Peter Lassen emigrated to America in 1831 from his native Denmark. He settled in Missouri, where he practiced his trade as a blacksmith. In August 1840 he arrived at Sutter's Fort, but soon departed for San Jose. A year later he moved back to the Sacramento Valley, where he worked a small ranch and did some blacksmithing work for Sutter. In 1844, he acquired the 22,000-acre Rancho Bosquejo on Deer Creek (Tehama County) as a land grant. Hoping to sell farmland to the new immigrants he was leading from Missouri in 1848—and hearing of the gold discovery en route—he blazed a new trail to his ranch through wild, mountainous terrain and around endless volcanic peaks. By 1855 he had sold the ranch and relocated to the Honey Lake region, not far from Susanville. While searching the Black Rock Desert for a "lost" silver mine in 1859, Lassen was killed by an unknown assailant. Lassen County was created in 1863. Lassen Peak, Lassen Emigrant Trail, Lassen National Forest, Lassen College in Susanville, Lassen Volcanic National Park, Lassen High School in Susanville, and a junior high school in Sacramento are all named for him.

Leidesdorff Streets in Folsom and San Francisco

William Alexander Leidesdorff was a wealthy merchant sea captain who sailed to California as master of the *Julia Ann* in 1841. He became prominent in San Francisco civic affairs, and was appointed U.S. Vice-Consul to Mexican California. As the grantee of the 35,000-acre Rancho Rio de los Americanos, he came to Sutter's Fort in 1846 to inspect his new holdings. Captain Sutter accompanied him on the tour, both grandly clad in their military dress uniforms. William Leidesdorff was born in St. Croix, Virgin Islands, in 1810 to a Danish father and a mixed-race mother, and died in San Francisco in 1848. He is sometimes referred to as the "black founding father" of California.

Marysville, Yuba County

Founded in 1850 by Frenchman Charles Covillaud and his partners, the town was named for Covillaud's pretty wife Mary Murphy, a Donner Party survivor. Mary Murphy was married twice at Sutter's Fort, to William Johnson in June 1847, and to Charles Covillaud on Christmas Day, 1848. Mary Murphy Covillaud died in 1867, and is buried in the Catholic cemetery in Marysville.

Murphys, Calaveras County

Brothers John and Daniel Murphy, still in their early twenties, struck very rich gold here in 1848. The sons of Martin Murphy Senior, they were members of the Stephens-Murphy-Townsend Party that arrived at Sutter's Fort in December 1844. Murphys was initially known as Murphy's Diggings; later as Murphy's Camp.

Nicolaus, Sutter County

In 1843, John Sutter's friend Nicolaus Allgeier (sometimes spelled Altgeier) established a ferry to cross the Feather River on the road between Sutter's Fort and Sutter's Hock Farm. The town was established in 1850.

Reading's Bar, Shasta County

Once, hundreds of miner's tents were pitched on Reading's Bar—the site of a fabulous gold discovery made by Major Pierson B. Reading in May 1848. Reading's gold finds here and on the Trinity River opened the entire northern regions of California to the Gold Rush. Today Reading's Bar exists only as California Registered Historical Landmark No. 32, a stone and brass monument erected on Clear Creek Road.

San Martin, Santa Clara County

In a roundabout way, San Martin takes its name from Martin Murphy Senior, the patriarch of the large Murphy clan who came to California in 1844 as part of the Stephens-Murphy-Townsend Party. Mr. Murphy and his five sons were with John Sutter's army in the Micheltorena campaign in early 1845; afterward Murphy took his unmarried children to Santa Clara to settle. He built the first Catholic church in the area, naming it for his patron saint, St. Martin of Tours, and the town that developed adopted the church's name. Two of his sons founded Murphys in Calaveras County.

Schallenberger Ridge, Placer County

Moses Schallenberger was only seventeen when he spent the winter of 1844-45 alone in a hastily erected log cabin at Truckee (Donner) Lake. Unable to follow his two companions out on foot when food became scarce, Schallenberger stayed to guard six wagons belonging to the Stephens-Murphy-Townsend Party after the other five wagons had been successfully taken over the pass. He was rescued on March 1, 1845, and taken to Sutter's Fort with others of his wagon company who had been snowbound on the South Yuba River. Moses Schallenberger became a leading figure in ranching and politics in San Jose, living until 1909. The 7,469-foot high, 1,923-acre ridge named in his honor, clearly visible from Truckee, towers over the south side of Donner Lake.

Sheldon, Sacramento County

Sheldon is a community on the southeastern edge of the city of Elk Grove, near the intersections of Grant Line and Wilton Roads. Established about 1860, it was named in honor of Jared Dixon Sheldon. Sheldon briefly worked at Sutter's Fort in the early 1840s, and was the grantee of Rancho Omochumnes in 1844, a property that spread from the modern Rancho Murieta development to Sloughhouse. The remnants of his gristmill, and a rebuilt replica of the Sloughhouse Inn—the stage stop he established in 1850—are on Highway 16, eighteen miles east of Sacramento. Both sites are registered California Historical Landmarks. Sheldon Road and Sheldon High School in Elk Grove are likewise named for Jared Sheldon.

Mt. Stephens, Nevada County and Stevens Creek, Santa Clara County

Although the creek's name is misspelled, both it and 7,254-foot elevation Mt. Stephens, near Truckee, are named for Elisha Crosby Stephens, captain of the 1844 Stephens-Murphy-Townsend Party. After serving in Sutter's army during the 1845 Micheltorena campaign, and Frémont's California Battalion as an ordnance mechanic during the Mexican-American War, Stephens settled in the Santa

Clara region on a 160-acre farm. Some years later he moved to Bakersfield, purchased 38 acres, and raised chickens and bees until his death in 1887.

Stockton, San Joaquin County

Stockton is a namesake city, albeit named for someone other than its founder. German-born Charles Weber, a member of the 1841 Bartleson-Bidwell Party, spent his first winter in California at John Sutter's New Helvetia settlement. The following spring, he established himself as a merchant in San Jose, and later purchased his business partner's interest in El Rancho del Campo de los Franceses, a 48,747-acre land grant in the San Joaquin Valley. Weber mined a small fortune in gold in 1848, but realized he could make a greater profit by selling supplies to other miners. He built and stocked a store on his property, and as the small village there blossomed into a thriving commercial center serving the southern mines, Weber founded the town he named Stockton, in honor of his Mexican-American War hero, Commodore Robert Stockton.

Sutter County; Sutter Buttes, Sutter County, and Sutter Creek, Amador County

Sutter County was one of California's original twenty-seven counties, established in 1850 upon statehood. The buttes, remnants of a volcano formed in the Pleistocene Epoch, were known as *los tres picos* (Three Peaks) in Mexican California. John Sutter kept a large flock of sheep at their base. The town of Sutter Creek, in the heart of the gold country, takes its name from the nearby creek. The creek is named for John Sutter, who mined for gold there in 1848. Sutter Creek is acknowledged as the general locale Sutter called "the piney woods," where he sent workers to whipsaw timber. Roads and schools throughout northern California are named for John A. Sutter.

Swift's Point, Glenn County

A warehouse is all that remains at the Sacramento River road crossing named for pioneer Granville P. Swift in the late 1840s. Swift crossed the plains to Oregon in 1843 and entered California the next year with the Kelsey Party. He served in Sutter's 1845 Micheltorena campaign, participated in the Bear Flag Revolt, and served as a captain in the California Battalion during the Mexican-American War.

Swift amassed a fortune during the Gold Rush. Legend has it that he buried his treasure about his adobe home; if so, it has never been found. California Historical Landmark #345 marks the location of the Swift Adobe, the first house built in Glenn County.

Todd Valley, Placer County

According to Hubert H. Bancroft's *History of California*, Todd Valley was named for Mary Todd Lincoln's nephew William Todd, the man who designed and constructed the Bear Flag at Sonoma in 1846. Another source gives the honor to pioneer Dr. F. Walton Todd, who opened a store there in 1849.

Yountville, Napa County

George C. Yount established this town in the early 1850s on the northern fringes of his Rancho Caymus land grant in the heart of the Napa Valley. He was the first permanent American settler in the Napa Valley; in 1846 his Rancho Caymus was the first Mexican land grant awarded there. Initially, Yountville was a small village, a six-block area with a public square. A former fur trapper whose meanderings brought him to California via the southern route in 1831, Yount died in 1865. He is said to be the first person to plant grapes in the Napa Valley. George Yount and John Sutter knew each other, but appear not to have had many business dealings.

PART II

RESTORATION

Years went by. Sacramento continued to grow during the 1860s and 1870s, though the denser centers of population remained west of Twelfth Street. On paper, the Fort's grounds had been divided into sixteen city lots, yet the surrounding neighborhood remained rural. A sprinkling of residences housed farmers and dairymen, and workers employed at the Sacramento Brewery on Twenty-eighth and M Streets. In the late 1860s, there were enough families to open a school on Twenty-ninth between J and K. During 1860-1880 occasional letters to the editors of various northern California newspapers suggested restoration of Sutter's Fort, but these roused no effective action.

The old Central Building was a curiosity, a suitable subject for young ladies, gathered beneath summer umbrellas, to practice art class lessons in sketching and painting. In January 1881, a Convention of Pioneers met in Sacramento to discuss possible methods of honoring the memory of the recently deceased Captain John Sutter. Some of them wanted a simple monument; others a memorial chapel. Still others wanted to restore the old Fort. In April 1887, the Women's Relief Corps proposed that Sacramentans subscribe to a fund to purchase the former Fort property, and then donate the site for a home for invalid wives and widows of army and navy personnel. Nothing happened. The pioneer convention's ideas somehow lapsed in committee, and the ladies' proposal fizzled.

In 1888 the Native Sons of the Golden West, a fraternal organization formed in 1875 of men born in California who were dedicated to preserving the state's colorful history, received a proposed resolution from member Carl E. Grunsky of Sacramento Parlor 26:

> *There is no spot in California more closely associated with the history of the pioneer days of this state than Sutter's Fort. It commends the veneration of all Native Sons of California, and it is the duty of our organization to perpetuate the memories associated with the spot and to preserve the site of the fort from further desecration;*

therefore be it resolved, that a committee... be appointed... to devise ways and means for the restoration of Sutter's Fort and its permanent preservation.

Although the resolution was accepted, the Native Sons had not yet taken action when, in mid-1889, Sacramento's board of city trustees decided to open Twenty-seventh Street from K to L. The cut-through would necessitate the destruction of the decaying Central Building, the only standing remnant of Sutter's Fort. Within days of the trustee's announcement, a patriotic and well-known Sacramentan named James G. Martine sent an open letter to the *Sacramento Union*, addressed "To the Pioneers of the Pacific Coast." Excerpted sections of his letter reads:

In the year '49, and even before that date, you left home, friends and all that was dear to you, and journeyed to the shores of the broad Pacific in search of fame and fortune. After many months of toil and hardship you finally reached her golden shores, both tired and hungry.

Pioneers, do you remember how grateful you felt then for the shelter given you by Sutter's Fort? Well, gentlemen, that was nearly forty years ago, and the old fort is still in the same place, but in a most wretched condition ... it is now old and can hardly stand, and unless you come to the rescue it will soon fall by the wayside.

I suggest that a subscription be raised among the citizens of Sacramento to purchase the ground and repair the old fort. The city authorities have already announced their intention of pulling it down unless something is done with it, and there is no time to lose.

Martine's letter was sent to newspapers throughout California, and to many newspapers in eastern cities. Small donations began pouring in: two dollars here, five dollars there. In January 1890, Martine reported that the local Sutter's Fort Fund, which was in the bank, amounted to $3,500. The Native Sons took charge of the project now, threw a benefit ball, and canvassed neighborhoods for more donations. Other organizations sponsored benefit picnics and concerts. In June Colonel C. F. Crocker, son of the late railroad mogul Charles Crocker, donated $15,000, and that fall Mrs. Leland

Stanford gave $500, with assurances from Senator Stanford that he would cheerfully subscribe whatever balance might be necessary to purchase the grounds of the old Fort. In November, the New England Associated California Pioneers of Forty-Nine sent a check for $100, a consolidation of its members' small individual donations.

Part of the problem from early on was the land owner Benjamin Merrill, whom James Martine, more than once, accused in print as holding out for a higher price. A series of indignant letters, written by him and others, appeared in newspapers nationwide. If the purpose was to embarrass Merrill into capitulating, it worked. In December 1889 Benjamin Merrill agreed to sell for $20,000, insisting that he had set this price very low and would not sell for that amount for any other purpose, as he believed that it was worth much more... and said he regretted that the newspapers had assumed he was unpatriotic. With the monies finally in place by October 1890, Merrill deeded the property to the Native Sons of the Golden West (NSGW). He also donated $2,000.

More was needed, of course, to begin the restoration. Fund raising efforts continued, while preliminary surveys commenced under the direction of NSGW member Carl E. Grunsky, a civil engineer who had recently executed improvements to the State Capitol grounds. The plan was to restore the dilapidated Central Building and rebuild the bastions and outer walls and, inasmuch as possible, rebuild the inner walls and partitions.

There was no trace left of the north wall and no one could find evidence of the east wall. Relying on such research materials as were available, as well as mistaken remembrances by aging pioneers, Carl Grunsky drafted a design. His ground plan included measurements of seventeen feet between outer and inner walls, the placements of the kitchen and distillery, and the unroofed corrals on both sides of the Central Building. He even outlined the location of the now nonexistent adobe east of the Fort that had housed Sam Brannan's store during the Gold Rush.

But neither Grunsky nor his fellow NSGW restoration committee members intended to restore outbuildings, or even replicate the structure as it had been in Sutter's time. Instead, they were creating a memorial to California pioneers.

Carl Grunsky had old city plat maps and old-timers' fading memories. He had the Central Building as a reference point. He had

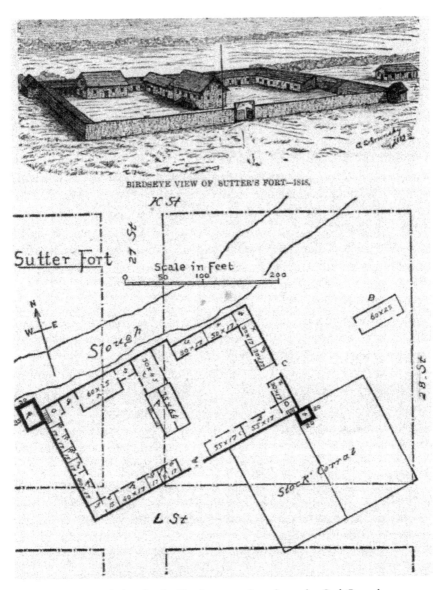

BIRDSEYE VIEW OF SUTTER'S FORT—1846.

The ground plan for the Fort's restoration, drawn by Carl Grunsky.
Author's collection.

conflicting reports of the Fort's dimensions from published sources such as Hubert Bancroft's *History of California,* Lansford Hastings' *Emigrant's Guide,* and Edwin Bryant's *What I Saw in California.* He did not have a ground plan of the original Fort, although such a diagram existed. It would not be found until the mid-twentieth century—and when it was, it would offer proof that the reconstructed Fort was much smaller than the one John Sutter built.

The Fort's last blacksmith Ephraim Fairchild, still residing in Sacramento, helped Grunsky find the coal pit in the west yard and, thereby, the southwest corner of the original structure. Problems arose when careful measurement determined that this corner would extend into the middle of the proposed L Street alignment. Development of private residences had already started along K and Twenty-eighth Streets, but as yet there was no development along the portion of L Street that bordered the Fort's south side. To allow for reconstruction of the southwest corner, state and city governments approved agreements which would be finalized with a future land swap.

Grunsky's plan was approved in 1890. Although he had been the one to initially propose the restoration of Sutter's Fort to the Native Sons, had conducted preliminary surveys, drawn preliminary plans, and been appointed as a Sutter's Fort Trustee, a man named James Seadler was the actual architect, and superintendant in charge, of rebuilding the Fort.

Mr. Grunsky now stepped away from the project, to devote his time and energies to his other commitments and interests. Carl Grunsky had been the chief assistant engineer for the State of California from 1879 to 1888. His specialties were in irrigation, river rectification and drainage issues. During the years the Fort was being reconstructed, he was a consulting engineer to the Commissioner of Public Works and a member of the state's Examining Commission on Rivers and Harbors. Afterward he held several prestigious positions, among them city engineer of San Francisco, and as a member of the Isthmanian Canal Commission.

In early 1891 the State of California appropriated $20,000 toward the restoration, and the first brick of the new wall was laid on the afternoon of September 22, 1891. According to the *San Francisco Call*, "Old-time methods have been followed in the manufacture of [the] adobe bricks."

But money was tight, and by that time kiln-fired bricks were far cheaper than the cost of labor-intensive manufacture of sun-dried mudbricks. The Fort's exterior walls were rebuilt with rust-colored, kiln-fired brick two and a half feet thick, in agreement with Sutter's recorded statements; and the Central Building was patched with the same. To stay within budget, the outer walls rose only fifteen feet high instead of Sutter's original eighteen feet. For the same reason, the reconstructed bastion walls were two and a half feet thick, instead of the five-foot thickness noted by both Sutter and Lansford Hastings. Adobe bricks were used in the reconstruction of many (but not all) of the inner walls; but these, too, were shorter than the estimates provided by pioneers who had once lived at the Fort.

The Native Sons did not reconstruct Sutter's original three-room adobe adjacent to the Central Building, nor did they rebuild the large adobe-walled threshing enclosures and corrals which abutted the exterior south wall. Also missing from the reconstruction were the several small wooden buildings and sheds that Sutter had erected in the courtyards. The largest of these, standing in the southwest corner, was the original blanket factory, which Sutter himself had relocated against the north wall before 1847.

During the reconstruction the entire knoll (except for the Fort's interior) was graded. This process, completed in 1891, largely compromised any future archeological value of the grounds. Site grading included an oval-shaped excavation on the northwest side, as the start of a proposed artificial lake meant to represent the now partially filled-in, partially other-directed slough. As of 1897, the excavation still yawned; authorities viewed the water-filled hole as an eyesore and a mosquito-breeding swamp.

Although both Carl Grunsky and James Seadler knew that all of the original roofs had been shaked, budget considerations meant that donated Spanish tiles were used instead. The so-called Kyburz Annex (built to simulate Sutter's home in Switzerland), with the adjoining kitchen and distillery, were added on the north and west sides of the Central Building. The walls were covered with protective concrete plaster, and whitewashed.

The total cost of the reconstruction work amounted to $55,890. In its 1892-93 session the California legislature appropriated another $15,000, bringing the state's total contribution so far to $35,000. The balance was raised by subscriptions. Fifteen subscriptions were for amounts in the hundreds or thousands; the majority of donations ranged from fifty cents to fifty dollars.

On April 26, 1893, the Sutter's Fort Memorial Monument/California Pioneer Memorial was dedicated with eloquent prayer and bombastic oratory on a delightful spring day with a cool fresh breeze blowing from the south—notwithstanding that the restoration was not quite finished. Speaker Thomas Flint, a state senator and Grand President of the Native Sons, said he hoped that in a short time the committee in charge of the project would be able to complete the walls and other on-going work.

Festivities began at three o'clock from the Eleventh Street entrance to the Capitol, with a five-block long procession composed of Native Sons Parlors, some thirty members of the Sacramento Pioneer Society, marching bands, and hundreds of citizens in carriages. Several thousand people were already gathered in and about the grounds of the memorial. Battery B of the First Artillery Regiment, having preceded the other companies, fired a canon salute as the parade neared the Fort. Above the Fort and from all the buildings in the vicinity, the Stars and Stripes could be seen floating in the breeze. The ceremonies concluded with a short address by Mollie Johnson, Junior Past President of the Native Daughters of the Golden West, brief remarks from local pioneer Powell Lawson and past Grand President of the Native Sons R. M. Fitzgerald, and the Artillery Band's rendition of "America."

The corner that projected into L Street and the other work in progress was completed in 1894.

Sutter's Fort California Pioneer Memorial is the first large scale reconstruction and restoration of an adobe structure anywhere in the United States, and the largest memorial dedicated entirely to the memory of pioneers.

The Southeast bastion viewed from 28th and L Streets. *Photo by author.*

Subsequent Years

In September 1895 thirty thousand out-of-towners descended on Sacramento for the gala Great Electric Carnival, to celebrate the transmission of electricity to the city from the twenty-two mile distant Folsom Powerhouse. Thousands visited the Sutter's Fort Pioneer Memorial, where they listened to the music of a local band, strolled into rooms from which they imagined Gold Rush merchants had sold their wares, and viewed the few displays in the Central Building, now being used as a museum.

Slowly, the site became a repository for pioneer "relics." In March 1896 a newsman published a list of artifacts in the museum that he termed "meager": paintings of grizzlies and the steamer *Edward Everett*, an old stagecoach of the famous Pioneer Line, and an old covered wagon. Other items in the collection included James Marshall's saddle, a photo of the Folsom Powerhouse, a large assortment of Civil War paraphernalia, a saber that once belonged to Mariano Vallejo, John Sutter's candlestick, a gun carriage, and various miscellanies. The reporter ended with an appeal for more contributions because, he said, there was plenty of room for ten times more.

The public heeded his call. Books and documents, obsolete tools, ephemera, carts and wagons—even a huge hay press—were brought to the gates, where the resident caretaker turned nothing away. Wags began calling the restored Fort "Sacramento's Attic."

CAMP FORT SUTTER

At 5:15 on the morning of April 18, 1906, Sacramento residents were awakened by a seismic disturbance in the ground beneath their beds. The swaying, cradle-like movement, which seemed to pass from south to north, lasted a full minute. No one was hurt, and not one building was harmed. An hour later, despite the severance of direct telephone and telegraph lines to the Bay, they learned that San Francisco had been devastated.

The *San Francisco Call* reported that 200,000 destitute people were crowded together in Golden Gate Park. Survivors of the catastrophe needed food, shelter, jobs. Relief committees in San Francisco and Sacramento sprang into action with deliveries of food and supplies, distributed by boat and horse-powered wagons, because the gasoline in automobiles was considered too hazardous. By Sunday, April 22, refugees were flocking into Sacramento from San Francisco, Santa Rosa, San Jose and other stricken communities. "Capital City Now A Big Relief Camp," declared the *Sacramento Union's* headline. The question was, where to put them?

The first proposal was to create a camp at Sacramento's Agricultural Park, a huge facility that spanned B through H Streets between Twentieth and Twenty-third. The stables, sheds, barns, and storehouses, all new and well-floored, could accommodate 750 to 1,000 refugees—but there were no proper toilets for so large a number of people to actually reside there. After considerable debate, Sacramento's Committee of Seven, as the Executive Relief Committee became known, decided to use Sutter's Fort.

This choice was based on several reasons, one of which was sentimental. Historically, the Fort had been the first "relief station" in California. Of much greater import to the crisis at hand, Sutter's Fort was adjudged better adapted to the purpose because of its water supply, drainage, and other conveniences. Its walls and size made policing and cleanliness easier and there was plenty of room for tenting on the two large lawns in the courtyards. It contained "a bundle" of comfortable houses (the partitioned rooms along the

A drawing of the Fort when it served as a refugee camp for San Francisco
earthquake refugees in 1906. Note the still unpaved corner of 28th & L in
the foreground. *Author's collection.*

inside perimeter walls), and its location meant fewer complications in
transportation services.

Some electrical wiring was already in place, so by Wednesday,
April 25, outfitting of the Fort with lights and sanitary appliances was
progressing well. Forty-nine earthquake refugees had been lodged in
the Central Building the previous Monday, and two hundred more
were comfortably provided for on Tuesday night. As the *Union*
reported, all the old rooms within the walls were being floored and
fitted with wire cots and new mattresses, clean blankets, and cotton
sheets. A group of Sacramento ladies tidied up the second floor of
the Kyburz Annex with the intention of using the space as a hospital,
should the need arise, and the committee hired trained nurses to be
in constant attendance. Plans were to house women and children on
the second story of the Central Building's east side, with the northwest section of the Fort intended for women only.

Carpenters set to work building a kitchen in a south-wall room
near the L Street entrance, where one range had already been installed, supplemented days later with a French stove. An iron-stone
sewer line was laid from the L Street entrance east to Twenty-eighth
Street, extending to the alley between K and L. Large earth closets
(toilets) were dug on the still-unimproved grounds outside the Fort's

northeast side, to be filled in three times a week with fresh earth. The plan was to sink new ones as fast as the old were filled and disinfected. Outside the south wall, thirty-one men of the First Company of Signal Corps from Los Angeles set up in fifteen tents, to guard the camp and enforce discipline. Lights blazed from inside the enclosure, but inclement weather prevented the installation of a large tent in the west yard, intended for use as a dining pavilion.

Eighty-three refugees were lodged in the old rooms within the south and west walls, less than half of the 210 persons for whom beds had been provided. The long and narrow spaces were newly floored with rough lumber and divided into smaller apartments by rude partitions. A laundry room stood ready for use. Various local agencies provided simple but ample food: eggs, cereals, soups, beef and vegetables, breads, rice, and stewed prunes. "Sutter's Fort a Model Relief Camp," blared the *Union*'s headline on April 26, as the Fort's flag flew at half-mast to honor the earthquake's dead.

Yet all was not well. The refugees protested that they were subject to annoyances and indignities from visitors who stared at them as if they were curiosities in a museum. It was hard enough, they said, to lose everything by earthquake and fire without having to hold up their hats or papers in front of their faces to ward off the "vulgar gazes" of the inquisitive. They had no privacy! The visiting sightseers, on the other hand, took the position that they had a legal right to go where they pleased about the premises because the museum was a state institution.

The inmates' complaints provoked rumblings of both assent and disagreement from relief committee members. One of them told the visitors that the camp was not a menagerie; that the present case of emergency suspended the usual rules, and they were not to be allowed to pry about the living quarters. Another sided with the sightseers, saying that since the Fort was a public place, all citizens had a right to inspect it at will. In the end, the Committee of Seven voted to issue properly endorsed passes, and decreed that the public would be excluded on Sundays.

And there was more. Restrictions were imposed on the refugees. No inmate would be allowed to leave the grounds without a special permit, and the practice of early and late strolling about the city proper must cease. Further, all able-bodied male refugees were expected to accept the jobs that the committee procured for them.

Occupancy at the Fort camp fluctuated, then dwindled. Reports surfaced that a larger number of refugees were scattered about town instead of using the Fort's facilities.

By mid-May 1906, although it was still operative and had no plans to close anytime in the near future, Camp Fort Sutter was only serving one woman, one girl, and twenty-five men.

Camp Fort Sutter closed in June 1906. The structure was left in its improved state.

1900-1950: THE PIONEER MONUMENT

The state legislature's belated 1907 Act to officially accept Sutter's Fort from the Native Sons was a mere formality. In fact, they had agreed to take responsibility for the memorial on March 7, 1891, and to appoint a board of trustees who would be responsible for the preservation, protection, and improvement of the Sutter's Fort property.

Before 1900, the Board of Sutter's Fort Trustees had authorized expenditures for, among other things, refilling the excavated north-side slough area with 12,000 cubic yards of earth, $2,352; replacing broken roof tiles, $250; and paving two blocks of K Street with macadam, $1576. On January 1, 1899, the board's formal letter to Governor James Budd reported these and other 1897-98 costs, adding the recommendation that the state should make sufficient appropriations to improve and beautify the grounds around the Fort.

Beautification was coming. In January 1904, famed landscape engineer John McLaren, "on loan" from his duties as superintendent at Golden Gate Park, met with the Trustees of Sutter's Fort. He was awarded the contract for enhancing the grounds both inside and outside of the enclosure, and agreed to submit detailed plans in about two weeks. Meanwhile, the Trustees would go ahead with work already in progress, plowing the land so it would be ready for planting when McLaren's plans were approved.

John McLaren's idea was to plant trees only on the north, east, and west sides of the Fort because, at this time, the south side corner still projected into the mapped alignment of L Street. He advised that only native California trees and shrubs should be used. The trees were to be three different kinds of California oak, and those along K Street a deciduous variety, to avoid shutting the street off from sunlight in the winter months. Inside the courtyards, he planned to install clumps of California trees of different varieties, with graceful walks winding between them.

Several oaks were planted in 1904. The next year, the Sacramento Women's Council planted a number of palm trees on the east side of the Fort, along Twenty-eighth Street. This necessitated removing, on May 4, 1905, "three fine elm trees" which were thirty feet tall. Controversy flared, or so said the *Sacramento Bee*. However, those involved in the event—Governor George Pardee, city trustees, the Women's Council, Native Daughters of the Golden West, and the Sutter's Fort Board of Trustees—denied any conflict. John McLaren went on record as saying the Native Daughters had agreed with planting the palms between the newly-planted oaks. Governor Pardee mildly lamented the loss of those shady elms. Although there was some talk of removing them, the palm trees stayed where they were.

Between 1904 and 1908—but mostly after the Fort's service as a refugee camp for earthquake survivors ended—the Native Daughters added shrubs and spectacular rose gardens on the grounds, and a variety of fruit and nut trees in the yards inside the walls, which were still blooming into the 1930s.

In 1907, a smaller oval, in the same general area as the now filled-in 1891 north side excavation, became the commemorative pond (albeit without a sealed bottom) that had been envisioned during the Native Sons' reconstruction period. Also in 1907, according to an earlier agreement, the state purchased and officially gifted to the city enough property so that the city could reroute L Street in a southern curve around the park, bringing the state-owned Fort grounds to 6.2 acres. The east oval of the commemorative pond, this one concrete-lined, was constructed in 1909-1910. A four-foot-high safety fence was added around the two pond perimeters, as were sprinklers to aerate the water and maintain a constant depth of about sixteen inches.

Sometime in late 1909-early-1910, the Fort's gardener installed two five-foot long alligators, male and female, in the artificial ponds. In February 1910, an unknown vandal shot and killed "Mr. Alligator" with a rifle. The culprit wasn't found. Mrs. Alligator was removed to another facility, and the ponds' other occupants—a swan, some geese and a few ducks—reasserted their sovereignty.

Sycamores, willows, and coast redwoods eventually dotted the park grounds, most of them planted in the early 1900s. By the late 1920s, creeping vines covered the south wall, and magnificent wisteria framed the main gates.

The ponds on the north side of Sutter's Fort circa 1913, seen from K Street.
Author's collection.

A proliferation of robust city development sprang up on the streets surrounding the Fort's grounds. St. Francis of Assisi Catholic Parish was already there at Twenty-sixth and K Streets, having erected a church building in 1895, and dedicated a larger one on the same site in 1910. In 1916 Sacramento's Scottish Rite organization laid the cornerstone of its new temple at Twenty-eighth and L Streets, which opened the following year. The organization occupied the Temple until 1958, when a fire destroyed the building. Sutter Hospital opened for business in 1923, between Twenty-eighth and Twenty-ninth, with its doors facing L Street. In 1925 the Eastern Star Temple was completed near the corner of K and Twenty-eighth; and the Congregational Church at Twenty-seventh and L Streets was completed in 1926.

The State Indian Museum on the Fort's grounds, and the maintenance cottage east of it, were both completed in 1941.

In 1947 Sutter's Fort became a unit of the California State Park system.

THE FORT'S FIRST CURATOR,
HARRY PETERSON

When Harry Claude Peterson was named the Fort's first curator in 1926, he was well-qualified for the job: it was the type of work which had already absorbed much of his life.

In 1886, when Harry was ten, his family moved from Iowa to Mayfield, California because his father, Julius, had been hired as a superintendent for some of the construction at recently-founded Stanford University. In those early days, the Peterson family became personally acquainted with Leland and Jane Stanford. Later on, Julius Peterson was appointed the faculty member in charge of the forge at the university.

After graduating high school Harry clerked in a drugstore and dabbled in university classes, but spent more time indulging his passion for photography. He took his camera along as he

Harry Peterson, viewing relics at Sutter's Fort. *Courtesy California Room, California State Library McCurry Collection.*

bicycled the back trails in California, Oregon, Washington, Idaho, and Utah throughout the four years he spent as a typewriter salesman and book agent. During this time he became interested in the historical relics he saw on his travels.

Back home in Mayfield, (eventually annexed to, and consolidated with, Palo Alto) Harry helped his father move historical artifacts into the Stanford University Museum of Fine Arts. Mrs. Stanford was so moved by Harry's special interest in her late son's collections that in 1899, at the age of twenty-three, Harry Peterson was named curator of the university's art museum, despite his youth and incomplete college education. The job was supposed to be temporary, until they could find someone else. It lasted eighteen years.

Just before the 1906 San Francisco earthquake, Peterson had assisted with the cataloguing of 12,000 glass negatives of early California scenes photographed by Carleton Watkins. He took a few back to the Stanford Museum for conservation purposes, promising to come back to the city for more. Before he could return, the earthquake and fire destroyed the remaining negatives, and also caused the collapse of two wings in the Stanford Museum. Harry Peterson spent the next four years repairing thousands of art objects, thus gaining thorough experience in the conservation techniques of the time. He was also active in the California Historical Landmark League.

Life took an unexpected turn in 1917, when a new Board of Directors asked him to resign his curatorship at the Stanford Museum. Suddenly unemployed at age forty-one, Peterson had a wife and son to support. He was offered a position as curator of the Charleston Museum in South Carolina, but before he could get there he was drafted by the Army. After his discharge in 1919 he worked for the California State Library as a hands-on researcher, employment that took him throughout the mountainous regions of the old Gold Rush trails. His understanding of early California history grew. In 1920, the State Library hired him on a permanent basis as head of field research. He continued taking photographs, and published many historical feature articles in northern California newspapers.

Harry had a sense of humor. For the May 1922 "Days of '49" celebration in Sacramento, Peterson founded the Whiskerino Club, encouraging all men in the city to grow beards for the event. He joined the Ancient and Honorable Order of E. Clampus Vitus (ECV). Initially formed in California during the gold frenzy as a spoof on the distinguished Masons and Odd Fellows, ECV soon developed a more serious aim. As a benevolent organization, it donated or raised funds to aid needy gold miners, widows and orphans. In later decades the Clampers, as the members called themselves, declared an even more illustrious purpose: a dedication to the study and preservation of the heritage of California, especially its gold mining districts. Nonetheless, the spirit of having fun never diminished, and the Clampers delighted in playing sometimes elaborate, history-related hoaxes on each other.

Harry Peterson played host to the new local chapter when it gathered for a meeting at Sutter's Fort on February 22, 1936. Just before the evening's scheduled entertainment—a playlet entitled "Although His Hair Was White as Snow, He Still Had One Wild Oat to Sow"— Harry stood to make "an historical announcement."

He said he had been in San Francisco on April 18, 1906, the day of the great earthquake. As frantic soldiers dynamited buildings along Market Street in a vain attempt to stop the fire from spreading, he had begged a commanding officer for one last look inside the Society of California Pioneers' headquarters at Fourth and Market Streets. Just before he was shoved out by explosive-carrying soldiers, he was able to grab a large rag from a tottering case.

Now, before his 1936 Clampers audience, Harry unfurled the rag and, with a flourish, displayed the *original Bear Flag of 1846*! Cheers rent the roof, and of course Peterson was lauded to the skies. But when Harry solemnly proffered the organization's requisite documentation, his prank was exposed. The parchment he produced bore the cleverly falsified signatures of men who had been part of the Bear Flag Revolt along with others whom the Clampers very well knew had *not* participated. The members had been conned, if only briefly. High hopes to the contrary, the Bear Flag had indeed been destroyed in the 1906 fire.

Harry's Historical Museum

Harry Peterson's vision for the Fort as a historical museum— rather than simply a pioneer memorial—was grand, and he had funding. Two years earlier, Assembly Bill 610 had authorized $10,000 to reorganize and preserve the collections at Sutter's Fort. Peterson's list of proposed exhibits spanned the years from 1839, the year of John Sutter's arrival, through 1869, the completion of the first transcontinental railroad.

Harry urged the restoration of historic rooms: Sutter's private apartments, the distillery, the blacksmith shop, and James Marshall's woodworking shop. During his tenure as curator he built the open wagon sheds along the north wall, had many shed (perimeter) rooms floored in simulated adobe, installed partitions in them, and shaked the shed roof sections as they had been in Sutter's time.

All the same, his interests centered on the Gold Rush years, and he soon conceived the idea of turning the memorial into a treasure house of 1849 mementoes. Moreover, after the original monies awarded by the state were used for initial upgrades, Harry was left to his own ingenuity. His displays mainly featured those artifacts dealing with the period between the gold discovery and the coming of the railroad, despite the fact that the Fort's founder, John Sutter, no longer owned the property for most of that period.

The average annual attendance of about 400 tourists by 1925, jumped to over 2,500 during 1926, after Harry opened the Fort as a "Days of Forty-nine" museum.

The Fort as Harry Peterson saw it. Note the ornamental trees in the interior yards, foundation plantings, and the ivy-covered exterior south wall with a profusion of wisteria around the gate. St. Francis Church is in the background.
Author's collection.

1939 Centennial Celebration

Definitely, the capstone of Peterson's career at the Fort was the 1939 centennial celebration of Sutter's landing on the American River. Called the Sacramento-Golden Empire Centennial, or California's Fiesta Year, fifteen northern counties participated in a four-month celebration, scheduled from May 1 through August. The state allocated $25,000 for further restorations at the Fort.

By this time the oval pond outside the north wall with its rustic bridge and fence, representing the former slough, had been in place for over a decade. Inside the walls Peterson spruced up rooms, and the courtyard exhibits—the three Concord stagecoaches, the cannons, and the very tall, narrow 1850s freight wagon. Donated to the Fort in 1894, this wagon had been built to specifications for a gold-rusher-turned-entrepreneur named Charles Huffman, who used twelve mules to haul it. Harry brought in massive bleached oak display cases to install in the Central Building, and to line the western sections of the inner walls. These were filled with tastefully arranged, genuine artifacts from the 1840s–1860s: mining equipment, hair wreaths, music boxes, household furnishings, photographs, and diaries. Other true treasures he displayed were the buckskin coat Pierson Reading was wearing when he arrived at the Fort in 1843; James Marshall's saddle, his carpenter tools and his wooden gold pan; and the old printing press Sam Brannan had brought out on the *Brooklyn* in 1846.

One 1939 financial report, detailing proposed expenditures for the centennial, listed rehabilitation costs of $500 for Sutter's rooms, $450 for the blacksmith shop, $850 for miner's stores, and $250 for cannon remounting. All rooms were refurbished as it was supposed they had looked in the summer of 1848, allowing the park to showcase certain rooms Sutter would have used before the gold discovery, as well as those changes effected by the Gold Rush. Preliminary work, essential before any fitting up of the rooms could begin, was finished by February 1939. This included shaking the roofs at a cost of $7,000, another $4,500 for preparing the entire west end as exhibition rooms, and some permanent adobe brickwork. In all, 10,000 bricks were used to construct walls, partitions, door sills and walkways.

Several truckloads of cottonwood and willow trees were cut down on the American River and brought to the Fort, to be split to furnish lumber for hand-made period furniture. A large brick forge was installed in the blacksmith shop, and existing fireplaces were rebuilt, all in working order and not just facades. The interior walls, still covered by the whitewashed concrete plaster from the 1890s restoration, were "antiqued" by various methods, as were the doors and floors. A blacksmith created typical hardware from the 1840s for the doors and fireplaces. A number of old European barrels were purchased, as were ten to fifteen cowhides for chair coverings, and a fine bear skin for the reconstructed saloon. Exhibits in the stage coach and wagon sheds were rearranged. The Fort was closed during parts of the process.

Ceremonies at Sutter's Fort on Sunday, April 30, kicked off the Golden Empire festivities in Sacramento. Spectators—bearded men in red shirts and hoop-skirted women—watched while Governor Culbert Olson and other officials opened with the obligatory speeches. Commemorative plaques, mounted on the south wall of the Central Building, were dedicated. Two were bronze. One came from the government of Switzerland, and the other from the citizens of Lititz, Pennsylvania, where John Sutter spent his last years and was buried. By far the largest, at nearly five feet tall, was the Sutter Plaque, a limestone and marble bas-relief created by artist Carlo Taliabue, a gift from the Native Sons and Daughters of the Golden West.

Musicians strolled the grounds. Characters representing John Sutter, James Marshall, Kit Carson, Bret Hart, pony express riders and other pioneer figures re-enacted early events. Just inside the main gates celebrants were greeted by a hay press, a great wooden device built by farmer A.J. Weldon in Plumas

The Hay press on display at the Centennial Celebration. *Courtesy Library of Congress.*

County, in 1868. Its hand-carved, huge corkscrew was powered by horse or mule to compact cut grass into hay bales. A few steps away stood the tall fire bell tower from Young America #6, one of Sacramento's early volunteer fire stations. A newspaper room, complete with old hand presses, type cases, and specimens of California newspapers printed between 1846 and 1869, reminded sightseers that the *Placer Times*, Sacramento's first newspaper, published its first edition at the Fort in 1849.

The Native Sons and Daughters Room held objects of early days. Other rooms depicted Sutter's private quarters, his bedroom and adjoining kitchen. A Pioneer Gallery in the distillery building drew appreciative comments, as did the Fort's large collection of pioneer-era firearms. Perhaps the most popular display was a replica of Peter Slater's 1848-49 saloon, featuring a crude bar, old bottles, and gaming tables.

Those were the most prominent exhibits, but there were others: 1850s man-powered fire engines, mounted cannon, carts, gold mining equipment, and still more rooms furnished with paraphernalia designed to give visitors a peek back in time to the Sutter years and the Gold Rush era.

On July 19, 1939, during the four-month Sacramento-Golden Empire Centennial, the Native Sons and Native daughters of the Golden West planted a European Oak in the Fort's east yard. Also known as a Turkey Oak, the tree was from Kandern, Baden, Germany, the Black Forest region where Sutter was born.

During his last years as curator, Harry lived in a snug little one-bedroom apartment inside the Fort, north of the east gate. His wife, Lillian, continued to reside in their home in Palo Alto. The apartment was complete with bedroom, bathroom, kitchen, sitting room and fireplace, but the only telephone was in his office on the second floor of the Central Building. On January 23, 1941, Harry suffered a heart attack while inside his apartment. Crawling through a rainstorm and upstairs to his office, he phoned his physician. Unfortunately, the gates were locked from the outside, forcing Harry to crawl to a point where he could throw the keys over. The doctor rushed him to Mercy hospital, where he died later that day. A memorial service, attended by several hundred friends and dignitaries, was held in Sacramento on February 9.

Harry Peterson was succeeded by historian Carroll D. Hall, who served as curator 1941-1953. Carroll Hall authored *Donner Miscellany*, a 1947 publication of the Book Club of California.

Harry's Assistant Virginia Storti

Virginia might very well have aided and abetted Harry Peterson with his Bear Flag hoax. She was hired as registrar of the Sutter's Fort collections, to help Harry organize and catalogue the vast collection of artifacts which had been stored at the Fort for decades. It was an immense task, one for which Virginia had little experience, although she had previously helped Harry catalogue materials at the Marshall Museum in Kelsey. She began her duties by stamping "Property of Sutter's Fort" on every piece in the collection, then writing an accession number in ink on each.

Over the next several years Harry taught her to be a skilled museum technician. Upon his death she assumed the role of curator, but the top position was not to be hers for long. Despite Harry's mentoring, and her own in-depth familiarity with the collection, she was appointed assistant curator in September 1841, after Carroll D. Hall was hired as curator.

She was a native Californian, born in Tehama County in 1894 as Virginia Rollins. Virginia was always proud of the fact that her great-grandparents, Mr. & Mrs. John Augustus Chase, had settled in Tehama County as pioneers in 1852. Following her education at a California high school and a business college, she enrolled in Columbia University. During World War I she was a private secretary to high-level British and Canadian statesmen, in New York.

Returning to California, Virginia worked for a time as a fashion model in a San Francisco department store before becoming a temporary aide to Harry Peterson in 1930, at the James Marshall Museum in Kelsey. Soon thereafter, she came to the Fort as a full-time employee. In the late 1930s Virginia married Attilio E. Storti, a World War I veteran who was employed by the state division of architecture.

As assistant curator, Virginia co-authored, with curator Carroll D. Hall, the 1944 booklet "Sutter's Fort Historical Museum." She retired in June, 1950, and was feted at a going-away luncheon in Sacramento's Tuesday Clubhouse. Virginia Rollins Storti died October 28, 1965. She was survived by her husband, and her mother.

THE GREAT DISCOVERY:
THE KÜNZEL MAP

The Native Sons of the Golden West didn't have it when they restored Sutter's Fort in the 1890s. Harry Peterson didn't have it when he renovated the Fort for the 1939 Centennial. Neither knew it existed, though it had been filed away in the archives of the Bancroft Library for generations. "It" isn't really a map. The Künzel Map is the ground plan of Sutter's Fort as it was in 1847, re-discovered through a chance encounter with a Midwestern professor who happened to be visiting Sutter's Fort in 1958.

Under Harry Peterson's stewardship, the Fort's exhibits centered on the California Gold Rush era with an emphasis on 1849, the most famous year. Peterson's successor Carroll Hall had continued with the same theme, with only slight modification. Then in 1953, California State Parks directed a new interpretive policy for all historical parks in the system: each facility was to limit exhibits and programs to telling the story of its own most significant historical years. For Sutter's Fort, this meant a change in focus to the years 1844-1849, when its founder and builder was still its central figure. Displays, buildings and landscaping were to portray the Sutter Period as nearly as could be determined by new research.

Of course, the early months of the Gold Rush *were* still relevant to the new directive, since several shop and saloon keepers had rented space inside the Fort beginning in 1848, but extensive study of the Sutter Period would take months. In the meantime, the state agreed to fund a complete inspection of the Central Building, and, if necessary, make repairs.

In compliance with the new interpretive policy, monument superintendent Carroll Hall prepared drawings for new exhibits in various rooms. The first change was to be a replica, in its exact dimensions and location within the walls, of the Priest, Lee & Company mercantile, which conducted business inside the Fort from the latter part of 1848 into the early months of 1849. The plan was that once their proper location was found, the relative placement of other 1848-49 businesses could be ascertained, and appropriate displays designed. State Parks historian H. Eugene Rensch was given the research assignment, and began his study in the summer of 1954. His path would take him far afield of merely finding the locations of the various 1848-49 shops, saloons, and flophouses.

Mr. Rensch pored over the museum's on-site files, and period maps at the State Library. Sources contained many conflicting statements, and almost no two agreed on the Fort's dimensions. His next step was to collect the property deeds associated with Sutter's Fort, those bestowed by August Sutter to store and hotel keepers from December 1848 through March 1849, the basic deeds from which six or seven lines of title were ultimately derived through 1869. There were dozens of Sutter deeds at the County Recorder's Office, both for sales of areas inside the Fort, and for other transfers of properties throughout the new city of Sacramento. All had to be examined, and the Fort deeds winnowed out.

Disappointingly, not one of the Sutter deeds gave an exact dimension, instead providing only indications of general divisions and uses of rooms within the Fort. Mr. Rensch went back to the Recorder's Office, to obtain subsequent documents evidencing sales or rentals from the original buyers to others. In these he found only two that contained exact measurements in feet and inches. All other deeds regarding spaces within the Fort were worded in typical nineteenth century fashion. For example, "That row of adobe buildings... on the South side... and East of the large gateway on the South... Also the short row of adobe buildings and the bastion at the corner... being at the East end of said row of buildings first above described and South of the gateway at the East end of said Fort." And so forth.

Comparing the deeds with early city survey maps, later city plat maps, and the Native Sons' ground plans prepared for the 1890s restoration, Rensch began to construct a color-coded ground diagram. His goal was to fit the known renters and buyers of 1848-49 into their proper locations.

Over time Mr. Rensch's diagrams and comparisons and findings became quite complex, filling a twenty-page typescript report. It became apparent to him that the trading post Sutter built had to have been much larger than the Native Sons' reconstructed Fort. Accumulating evidence suggested that the original southeast bastion had been over one hundred feet east of its placement in the 1890s restoration, which meant that the original east wall had extended all the way to Twenty-eighth Street. Moreover, based on Rensch's analysis, the original north wall—all trace of which had vanished during the 1861-62 monster floods—had to have been a good twenty feet farther north.

It was a stunning outcome, and yes, he did find the location of the Priest, Lee store within the quadrangle, but there were still tantalizing pieces missing—the true lines of walls, and precise dimensions of overall size. Mr. Rensch didn't have time to pursue the matter. Reassigned to other research projects at Colombia Historic State Park, and the proposed restoration of Sacramento's historic waterfront, he was absent for three years.

On his first day back at Sutter's Fort in August 1958, an unexpected visitor arrived. This was Dr. Ralph P. Bieber, a professor at Washington University in St. Louis, and a noted historian of the American West. During a conversation that morning, Dr. Bieber mentioned that he had once seen a plan of the Fort in a German pamphlet in the Bancroft Library at the University of California, but he could not remember the name of the author.

It was a lead—one that Eugene Rensch had previously seen in a bibliographical index listed only by title, but hadn't had time to investigate. Dashing back to the Bancroft Library on his next day off, he at last found the obscure promotional pamphlet entitled *Upper California, A Geographical Description*, published by Dr. Heinrich Künzel in Darmstadt, Germany, in August 1848.

And there it was: the priceless *grundriez*, or ground plan, of Sutter's Fort circa 1847—to scale.

It showed everything historians knew or supposed about the Fort in Sutter's time: the massive corrals outside the south wall, Sutter's first three-room house once adjacent to the Central Building and the corral north of it; the well, the slough, the small gate in the north wall, the exact sites of the distillery, kitchen, outdoor oven, gristmill, and so on. Each room or area on the plan was numbered, with a corresponding title in German. It is the only source that definitively locates, as well as designates the sizes and uses of, the divided rooms between the outer and inner walls as they were before the Gold Rush.

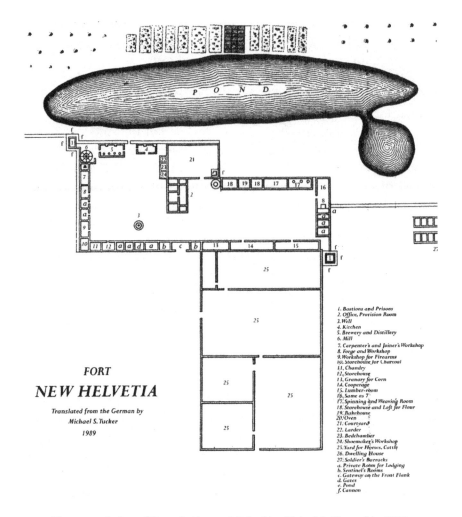

1. Bastions and Prisons
2. Office, Provision Room
3. Well
4. Kitchen
5. Brewery and Distillery
6. Mill
7. Carpenter's and Joiner's Workshop
8. Forge and Workshop
9. Workshop for Firearms
10. Storehouse for Charcoal
11. Chandry
12. Storehouse
13. Granary for Corn
14. Cooperage
15. Lumber-room
16. Same as 7
17. Spinning and Weaving Room
18. Storehouse and Loft for Flour
19. Bakehouse
20. Oven
21. Courtyard
22. Larder
23. Bedchamber
24. Shoemaker's Workshop
25. Yard for Horses, Cattle
27. Soldier's Barracks
a. Private Room for Lodging
b. Sentinel's Rooms
c. Gateway on the Front Flank
d. Gates
e. Pond
f. Cannon

FORT

NEW HELVETIA

Translated from the German by
Michael S. Tucker
1989

The ground plan of Sutter's Fort published by Heinrich Kunzel in 1848, with English translations. Note the huge corrals in front of the main gate, and the immigrant barracks at upper right. *Courtesy Sutter's Fort.*

The restored Fort measures 320 feet long from west to east. The west end is 163 feet wide, while the east end measures 137 feet, a result of the truncated north wall east of the Central Building to accommodate the contours of the slough, as Sutter himself had done in the 1840s. The east wall of the distillery, once 72 feet west of the Central Building, is only 25 feet distant today.

The measurements in Künzel's *grundriez* proved that the present-day Fort is only two-thirds the size of the structure Sutter built.

It also stipulated the seven original room divisions inside the Central Building. Since that building was already undergoing repairs at the time Künzel's publication was found, the two open upstairs rooms from the 1890s restoration were modified to showcase Sutter's office and "parlor," the clerks and doctors offices, and the dining room. But who was Dr. Heinrich Künzel, and how did he get Sutter's ground plan?

Dr. Heinrich Künzel

Born in 1810, Heinrich Künzel grew up to become a prominent man in many social and professional circles. As a youth he studied languages, graduating with honors from the most advanced secondary school system in Germany. He became a medical student, then changed to theology and philosophy, earning a doctorate. He was a professor of history, and German and English literature, at the Polytechnic School in Darmstadt, while simultaneously teaching English to Princess Marie of Hessen, later Empress of Russia.

Künzel contributed to important scholarly publications, but also was an advocate for common causes. In the early 1840s the German states were simmering with social and political unrest, which eventually led to the revolutions of 1848-49. Strife at home made potential opportunities elsewhere seem brighter, and therefore aroused considerable interest in the frontier regions of the United States. After 1845, Künzel was active in behalf of German emigration. He co-founded a newspaper named *The German Migrant,* in addition to his duties as chairman of the Hesse Branch of the National Association of German Emigration and Settlement organization.

The situation in Europe, known throughout the world, did not escape the notice of John Sutter. From 1841 forward, he had been bound by the terms of his New Helvetia land grant to settle twelve families on his land. Marketing was a necessity, so Sutter sent a packet of promotional materials to the German emigration activist. Intrigued, Künzel researched the recently published reports of John Charles Frémont and Lansford Hastings, among other sources. The result was a pamphlet, written to inform Germans who were thinking of emigrating to California.

Upper California contained two illustrations: Sutter's ground plan of the Fort and a map of his land grant, delineating boundaries, rivers, and other features. In his Preface, Dr. Künzel stated that both maps were prepared from original drawings provided by Captain Sutter. Heinrich Künzel was very impressed by his fellow country-man's success. "To be true he is a Swiss," said Künzel, "but a German Swiss who originally stems from the Basel area... He has shown what German, Swiss energy and strength of character can accomplish."

Europeans were aware of the American conquest of California, but as of the date of the pamphlet's publication, had not yet received word of the gold discovery. Certain of the passages in *Upper California* read as if the words came from Sutter's own pen, combining fact with hyperbole as is typical of every businessman who advertises.

Needless to say, the 1958 discovery of the Künzel pamphlet and illustrations brought about a revolutionary change to the entire future of restoration work at Sutter's Fort, and its historical interpretation and exhibits. Archeological excavations in 1959 confirmed the validity of Künzel's diagram and in fact found evidence of a second well, a feature alluded to in the Fort's logbook during Sutter's time.

CHANGING TIMES AND EXHIBITS

By California standards, Sutter's Fort is a very old building. Moreover, it is made of materials that don't stand the test of time without regular care and maintenance. Since it was reconstructed by the Native Sons in the early 1890s, displays and room exhibits have changed as ongoing research uncovers previously unknown facts, or because of changes in administrative policies concerning all of California's state historic parks, or when the exhibits themselves show signs of deterioration.

Throughout most of the twentieth century, the Fort as a pioneer memorial contained elements that were completely unknown to the pioneers who saw it in the 1840s—brick and concrete walkways and trees inside the courtyards, and park-like lawns surrounding the walls. In recent times the policy has been to restore the "look" of the Sutter Period, but for reasons of public health, as well as the safety and preservation of authentic artifacts, the site cannot be returned to exactly how it was in the 1840s.

In Sutter's time the Fort was an active trading post, with men, wagons, horsemen and draft animals coming or going every day. The grounds inside and outside the walls would have been a mix of bare earth and scattered tufts of trampled grasses. In summer, hooves and boots stirred up dust clouds; in winter, the ground turned to a muddy morass. Various native trees stood outside the walls, but there were no trees inside the courtyards when Sutter lived there.

Although a full-scale re-creation of the historic grounds is impractical, certain measures have been taken to create a more authentic ambiance.

The damaging vines and wisteria were removed in the 1950s, and the exterior walls resurfaced. Other invasive plants installed at the base of the walls in the early 1900s were removed, and the several ornamental trees and shrubs in the courtyards slowly disappeared through attrition and non-replacement.

Sometime between the end of World War II and 1955, the Spanish roof tiles on the Central Building, Kyburz Annex, distillery and kitchen, and the bastions were removed and replaced with pine shakes. The east gate was rebuilt in 1956.

In 1959, the interior of the Central Building was gutted, and steel rails were inserted to shore up about 50 percent of the original joists. After the interior was replaced, the building's south wall was refaced with a layer of adobe.

REHABILITATION 1980s-1990s

Beginning in the 1980s, Sutter's Fort acquired a different ambience from previous decades. Gone were the larger exhibits—the hay press, the stage coaches, the tall wooden freight wagon hauled by twelve mules, the fire engines and the fire bell—all removed to archival storage for their protection and preservation.

Although the state had rehabilitated many displays in the late 1950s, by the 1980s those room exhibits were aging, and in many instances, were considered more overly imaginative than historically accurate.

In cooperation with the California Department of Parks and Recreation, the Fort's dedicated docents embarked on a program of intensive study and research. The in-depth reports they submitted in the spring of 1984 covered every aspect of the 1840s decade, from socio-economic to cultural to political. They discussed the reasons for the surge in westward emigration, listing what tools and ordinary household items and medicines were available to pioneering families. Their reports contained floor plans and elevations, analysis of present-day visitor's probable impressions, how each separate room might relate to other Fort rooms, and cost estimates. Each report was appended with a bibliography of research sources. Many provided drawings and instructions to craftsmen for those items to be created by the rehabilitation teams or manufactured by outside contractors.

The Immigrant Room, displaying authentic replicas of period furnishings. *Photo by author.*

For those overlanders intent on settling in California, Sutter's Fort had been their initial destination. The goal now in the 1980s was for the Fort to appear, as much as possible, as it did when those immigrants arrived in 1845-47. The docents voiced recommendations for everything from appropriate period furniture to correct quilt patterns; tools and accessories for various shops, and the implements that Sutter's employees would have used in the kitchen and bakery. The bake oven, or *horno*, had already been rebuilt in October 1983, by local craftsmen who volunteered their time.

The rehabilitation work was scheduled to roll out in three long-range phases, with total anticipated costs of half a million dollars. To augment state funds, brochures soliciting donations were distributed. Plans called for the few decorative trees still inside the Fort (except for the European Oak in the east yard) to eventually be replaced with period-appropriate shelters of awnings or sheds. A trapper's Ramada and a covered saw pit were in place by 1986.

In May 1987, the Department of Parks and Recreation announced the debut opening of the Phase 1 refurbished rooms, set for June 1. Completed were the bakery, candle shop, carpenter shop, private living quarters, and the reconstructed carronade (the gun platforms at the main gate). Thus far, said the press release, about forty people in the Sutter's Fort Volunteer Rehabilitation Program had donated more than 30,000 hours to accomplish both the preparation and implementation of the plans approved in 1984.

Work on Phases 2 and 3 continued into the next decade. State funds and donations paid for the rehabilitation but the docents did most of the work themselves, except when it was necessary to hire a contractor, as it was for the basic structure of the period kitchen. No description of the original kitchen survives, except that it occupied a detached building on the north side, as seen on the Künzel Map. Therefore, the Volunteer Rehab Team's research for this room was intensive. A number of sources consulted yielded general data on fundamental cultural practices at historic frontier outposts; and more important, specifics on the employees and the culture at Sutter's Fort.

In John Sutter's day the kitchen prepared three meals daily for twelve to thirty men—and up to 150 men during planting and harvest seasons. It was built and equipped as a commercial-grade facility, not a more modest home kitchen. Most of the men employed as cooks at the Fort were English, French, or Americans who had been trappers or sailors before Sutter hired them. After studying hundreds of drawings and descriptions of shipboard cooking systems, 1840s European kitchens, and other frontier forts in America like Fort Vancouver, the team decided upon a European kitchen design with a large floor-level brick hearth, ovens imbedded in the brick walls, a kettle suspended by a built-in crane, a

Pots and crockery line the shelves in the first functional pioneer kitchen since Sutter's time. *Photo by author.*

"mush pot" with its own fire pit, overhead bars for hanging pots, and a warming shelf.

The pioneer kitchen was finished in late 1991. It is the first fully operational kitchen at the Fort since Sutter's time.

The Vaquero Room as photographed in 1991.
Courtesy Sutter's Fort.

The rehabilitation of other rooms saw completion during the early 1990s. The weaving and spinning room was re-fashioned as a working wool-weaving blanket factory, and furnished with looms and spinning wheels in a style reflecting the equipment James Marshall had manufactured in 1845. The existing blacksmith shop exhibit, which had not been changed since curator Harry Peterson installed the first display in 1939 for the Centennial Celebration, was upgraded to replicate the sights, sounds, and smells of an active forge.

Other displays were given face-lifts. In all, renovations at the Fort which were completed before the year 2000 comprised substantial sections of the interior rooms. Extensive as these makeovers were, however, they were not expected to last forever. Restoration, refurbishment, upgrading and updating will always be ongoing so long as the structure stands.

Replacing the Main Gate

In Sutter's time, according to the Künzel Map, the south-facing entrance was the *thor an der vorderseite*, the "front" or main entrance to the Fort. New south gates were installed in the 1960s. The style, though, bore scant resemblance to the best-known illustration of the Fort in 1847, a drawing by Lt. Joseph Warren Revere that showed Sutter's Indian guards being drilled outside, in front of the massive portals.

In time the inauthentic-looking, weather-worn 1960s gates were hardly more than a creaking, ineffective set of doors. With the help of Sutter's Fort volunteers, a new gate was designed, based on the details in Revere's drawing.

Many 1840s visitors described the Fort's "ponderous gates," but none described the materials from which the gates were made. While

The Fort's main gate, once again looking as it did in Sutter's time.
Photo by author.

the original date of installation is unknown, the south gates were in place when Pierson Reading arrived in late 1843, and it *is* known that Sutter considered the nearby oaks and jack pines to be inadequate wood for anything so large. In late 1841 he purchased Fort Ross, constructed of huge redwood planks, which Sutter dismantled and shipped to his settlement.

Since the Revere drawing shows that the south gates were constructed of continuous boards extending the full height of the walls, it is almost certain that the straight-grained redwood planks from Fort Ross were the materials Sutter used. The original gates, as depicted in the Revere drawing, swung from heavy columns and were stabilized by a heavy straight cross beam, surmounted by an arched cross beam bristling with spikes. This image became the new design chosen by State Parks officials. Redwood planks milled from trees downed on other state park lands were used as materials.

The construction project, a joint effort by State Parks and the California Department of Forestry, took three months. The builders, all inmates of the Growlersburg Conservation Camp—jointly operated by the California Department of Corrections and CAL Fire— quickly developed the types of skills required for all phases of the project, from milling lumber to constructing the footings and lintel.

Sutter's Fort filled with visitors during the popular Gold Discovery to Statehood Sesquicentennial in 1996. *Courtesy Sutter's Fort.*

Because the Growlersburg inmates built the gates, the cost was a fraction of what it would have been if the job had been given to a commercial contractor.

The massive, fifteen-foot, hinged redwood portals were raised into place on September 17, 1991 by a sixteen-man inmate crew using a gin-pole and block and tackle, just as Sutter would have done so many decades ago.

The Pioneer Wagon

Given that the majority of pioneers who came to Sutter's Fort trundled up to the gates in a covered wagon, what better exhibit could the Fort have than an authentic 1846 covered wagon to exemplify the pioneer era?

Yet when the idea surfaced in the late 1990s, and a committee of staff and docents was formed, the people involved found that it wasn't so easy because the only authentic pioneer wagons still around after 150 years were already in museums. After much discussion the committee decided to acquire a new wagon, authentically replicated. For six years the committee discussed, researched, and planned. They applied for— and after several frustrating delays were awarded—a state educational grant of $20,000. They sent out specifications to about six wagon makers, receiving widely varying estimates. The contract was given to Hansen Wheel & Wagon Shop in South Dakota, a firm that specialized in the construction or restoration of old west-style vehicles such as covered wagons, chuck wagons, buck boards, stagecoaches and other period conveyances. Hansen's price was $19,000.

The wagon arrived at the Fort on Monday, June 7, 2004, a masterpiece of hand craftsmanship in every detail, from the wagon box to its clouted axles, wheel hub boxing, and linch-pin hubs. The hardwood box of yellow poplar with hickory flooring was stained an aged blue-green, the running gear stained red, and all of the hand-forged hardware was coated in black. In keeping with known 1846 pioneer wagon details, it had no brakes, springs, or seats. In lieu of a standard 1846 tailgate, this one was hinged to let Fort visitors see inside, and to allow children to climb into the wagon bed while docents explained how it would have been packed for the trip west.

The wagon at Sutter's Fort is a replica of a typical farm wagon like the emigrants used, measuring 10.5 feet long by 45 inches wide, and adapted with bows to support a cover of heavy canvas or sailcloth which the travelers rainproofed with linseed oil or paint. Pioneer wagon covers usually had a flap in front and a puckering string in the rear, to help

The Fort's 1846-style pioneer wagon is a popular exhibit. *Photo by author.*

keep out rain and dust. Hollywood to the contrary, the pioneers did not use Conestoga wagons for their cross-continental journeys. Big-wheeled and boat-shaped, Conestoga wagons were the eighteen-wheelers of their time, designed to haul freight over New England roads and on the packed-earth Santa Fe Trail. They were pulled by specially bred teams of horses or up to twelve yoke of oxen (twenty-four animals). They were far too big and too heavy to traverse the Midwestern regions without sinking in prairie sands; too tall and bulky to cross the daunting Sierra Nevada.

Most people already owned a farm wagon. If not, they were relatively cheap at about $100. Smaller wagons kept the weight down—important when rolling over soft sands or urging draft animals up and over steep mountain terrain—because supplies, tools, and provisions for a six-month journey usually added up to two thousand or more pounds.

On the evening of August 21, 2004, the Sacramento Historic Sites Association and Sutter's Fort held a special "End of the California Trail Campfire and Western BBQ" with admission by advanced ticket purchase only, to celebrate the arrival of the 1846-style covered wagon. More than a hundred people attended.

Ongoing maintenance of the pioneer wagon is funded by public donations reserved for that purpose.

A ROYAL TOURIST

O n Friday, March 4, 1983, the staff and volunteers at Sutter's Fort State Historic Park were honored to receive a visit from Her Majesty Queen Elizabeth II. The Fort was one of the few places in California the queen had expressed a desire to see. Participants in the Fort's renowned Living History Program had planned and rehearsed an elaborate tableau, a re-creation of a typical day at Sutter's Fort in March 1846, when the Bear Flag Revolt, the American conquest of California, and the gold discovery were all still in the future. Approximately fifty Living History re-enactors were on hand to speak and act as if it were 137 years in the past.

The Fort was closed to the public for the day, yet hours before her scheduled arrival, a crowd ten people deep thronged the sidewalk in front of the Pioneer Church on L Street, hoping to get a glimpse of the British monarch. Members of the press were crammed into a cordoned-off viewing stand not twenty feet away from the main gates. On the lawns outside, bewhiskered members of the Kit

Queen Elizabeth II touring Sutter's Fort with guide Captain John Sutter. *Courtesy Sutter's Fort.*

Carson Mountain Men milled around a campsite display clad in buckskin, beads, and coonskin caps. Their wives and children, dressed in 1840s clothing, completed the scene of a wagon train stopping for provisions.

The queen's motorcade arrived promptly at 11:30 a.m. Her entourage, altogether some two dozen people including her husband Prince Phillip and her ladies-in-waiting, were all guarded by a swarm of Secret Service agents. Security was strict. Admission to the Fort was permitted by a State Parks pass only, issued to staff and volunteers weeks earlier.

Just before Queen Elizabeth stepped from her vehicle, an honor guard of thirty-five Kit Carson Mountain Men took their places in line along the entrance walkway. At the curb, State Resources Secretary Gordon Van Vleck officially welcomed the queen, and escorted her to the gates. Inside, the queen was greeted by State Parks Director Carol Hallett, and introduced to her host Captain John Sutter, portrayed by George Stammerjohan. Prince Phillip was introduced to his hostess, pioneer Mrs. Eliza Gregson, portrayed by Eileen Hook. Since their time was limited to a half-hour, the royal couple was given separate tours of the same exhibits, with more emphasis on gunsmithing and carpentry in his than in hers.

All of the rooms inside the walls were open, many occupied by costumed characters "going about their ordinary business" as backdrop scenery. Outside the cooper shop, a man was quietly earning his supper by weeding a vegetable garden specially cultivated for the queen's visit.

Six stations around the courtyards stood ready as planned stops of about four minutes each. At these stations hosts Captain Sutter and Mrs. Gregson explained the economics, politics and events of the time period, and the royals could ask questions of the players. Stations 1-3 featured ladies engaged in mending and sewing, cooks preparing foodstuffs at the outdoor kitchen and oven, and a cluster of tents occupied by unemployed "hangers-on" at the Fort. Between the tents and the next station, a vaquero was seen mending his saddle, carpenters sawed and hammered, a hatter and his wife were at work, a gunsmith repaired arms, and a laundress and candle-maker shared an open fire. Stations 4-6 were the blacksmith, gunsmith and carpenter shops.

To commemorate the occasion, the Sutter's Fort docents and members of the United Free Trappers Brigade (aka the Kit Carson Mountain Men), gave Queen Elizabeth a hand-made, fur-trimmed buckskin dress fashioned in the Sioux style. It was adorned with Blue Russian faceted beads, dew claws, quill wheels and seed heads, stitched on in over 113 hours of beadwork by Mark Dashnaw, who portrayed the Fort's carpenter. The smoking of the skins for the dress had been done at the Fort by docents Bob Sweedson and Bob Stewart, as was much of the sewing and fringing. The idea of making an Indian dress originated with docents Karen Catalano, a Comanche, and Gail Shortz. As protocol prevented presentation of the gift during the tour, the dress was delivered in advance to the British Consulate in San Francisco, which placed it aboard the royal yacht on the morning of the queen's visit.

At noon sharp the royal party departed the Fort, headed to the State Capitol for lunch with Governor and Mrs. Deukmejian before leaving Sacramento for a weekend in Yosemite. The Kit Carson Mountain Men gave the queen an orchestrated, rousing chorus of hurrahs as a send-off.

FORT TRIVIA

The pioneers who drove covered wagons to Sutter's Fort in the 1840s knew how far they had traveled, because they had odometers attached to their wagon wheels. These were simple, gear-driven devices that counted wheel rotations. Anyone with a little mechanical skill could make one from wood, although the most sophisticated odometers of the period were manufactured by scientific instrument makers using brass components. The circumference of the wheel and the daily rotation count enabled emigrants to calculate distance traveled with a high degree of accuracy.

———————

The year 1950 marked California's 100th anniversary of statehood. Sutter's Fort's curator Carroll D. Hall and Dr. Aubrey Neasham, regional historian of the National Park Service, created a traveling Centennial exhibit. Two white, blue and gold buses transported priceless artifacts to public venues, and as many schools as possible, throughout the state on a two-year tour. Among the rare items in the fourteen exhibit sections was the bill of sale that transferred ownership of Fort Ross to Captain John Sutter.

During the 1950s and 1960s, Sutter County Canning & Packing Company sold canned peaches, apricots, green beans, and other produce under the label "Sutter's Fort."

In May 1956, a never-before-seen exhibit opened. This was Sutter's jail on the ground floor of the southeast bastion, accessorized to appear as it might have looked in Sutter's time with straw on the floor, a wooden plate and tin cup, a cat o' nine tails, handcuffs, and leg irons.

Author Oscar Lewis published *Sutter's Fort: Gateway to the Gold Fields* in 1966.

Sutter's Fort State Historic Monument became Sutter's Fort State Historic Park on June 14, 1970.

The Park once had an resident cat named Anna. She gave birth to a litter of kittens in the northwest bastion on June 24, 1970.

On Sunday October 11, 1970, descendants of pioneers James and Eliza Gregson gathered at Sutter's Fort for a family reunion, and to commemorate their ancestors' arrival at Sutter's Fort on October 5, 1845. About one hundred Gregson descendants from all over the United States attended. Eliza Gregson's spinning wheel was on display at the Fort during Harry Peterson's tenure as curator, 1926-1941.

In the summer of 1971, a pregnant white burro named Maggie came to live at the Fort. Three months later she gave birth to a jack foal. All the children visiting the Fort that November day were quite excited with the newborn burro. In December, reporters and camera crews from Channel 10 were at the Fort to film the winner of the "name the burro" contest. The winning name was Milton Augustus, or "Gus" for short. Maggie left in June 1972 to be treated for an injury, but Gus stayed on for awhile.

In August 1975, the yet-again repaired *horno* (bee hive oven) cooked a batch of bread to perfection, to everyone's relief and satisfaction.

Governor Jerry Brown held a BBQ at Sutter's Fort on August 9, 1976. Senators, Assemblymen, department heads and the governor's staff and their families attended, numbering about three hundred in all.

Ceremonies for Mexican Flag Day at the Fort on February 24, 1977, drew 1,000 participants and spectators. Speeches, rope tricks, and exhibition dances entertained the crowd for hours.

The ancient cottonwood tree in the Park toppled in February 1978, after surviving for 140 years or more.

Sutter's Fort launched its acclaimed Living History Program in 1980, and its annual Mobile Living History Program, aka "River Trip" or "Trapper's Camp" in 1983. Trapper's Camp, held at two off-site camping grounds each October for schoolchildren, re-enacts an 1843 trapping expedition party sent out by John Sutter.

The city of Sacramento celebrated its 150th birthday in August 1989, with week-long festivities. Sutter's Fort hosted a gala all-day birthday party, with demonstrations and history skits, on Saturday, August 12. The climax of the Sesquicentennial was held at Discovery Park the following day, featuring a re-enactment of Sutter's landing. Costumed actors in rowboats were escorted by horn-blaring, siren-shrieking modern watercraft from the Sacramento Yacht Club.

Besides cats and burros, a family of barnyard chickens once roamed the Fort's courtyards. As late as 1990, two sheep lived in the corrals on the north wall.

In 1991, California State Historic Parks from San Diego to Sonoma paid homage to the state's Hispanic heritage. Sutter's Fort strung red and green ribbons on door lintels for the occasion.

The 100th anniversary of the Native Sons' Pioneer Memorial was celebrated as a special evening event at the Fort on Monday, April 26, 1993. Birthday cake was served.

California celebrated its Gold Discovery to Statehood Sesquicentennial in 1996, a state-wide commemoration of California's past from the gold discovery on January 24, 1848, to its admission as the Union's 31st state on September 9, 1850. From Death Valley to Sonoma, dozens of units of the Department of Parks and Recreation sponsored appropriate activities. Sutter's Fort State Historic Park held Pioneer Demonstration Days on August 17, 1996.

Television personality Huell Howser twice visited Sutter's Fort to film segments for his popular series *California's Gold*, in 2002 and 2007.

The Fort's east and south gates were both treated to a restorative "facelift" in 2014.

EPILOGUE

The structure John Sutter built in the 1840s has seen service as a frontier trading post, a private home, a refugee camp, a pioneer monument, a museum, and an authentic living history center. Sutter's Fort was registered as a National Historic Landmark in 1965, and listed on the National Register of Historic Places in 1978.

Reporters and cameramen from local television stations are regular visitors. The Fort has also welcomed crews from Reader's Digest, the British Broadcasting Corporation, and independent filmmakers. Descendants and distant relatives of John Sutter, or of other pioneers who worked at the Fort in the 1840s, show up fairly frequently—some arriving from as far away as Europe—to tour the facility and learn more about their ancestors.

Over the years hundreds of business and civic organizations, from law firms to historical societies, have chosen Sutter's Fort as a venue for after-hours receptions, banquets, and parties. Private groups have celebrated birthday or graduation parties inside the walls too, and have even held a few weddings.

Special fund-raising events sponsored by the Friends of Sutter's Fort Foundation occur periodically. One example is the June 2010 "Family Treasures: Collections of the Fort" benefit and silent auction. Attendees were treated to a private display of genuine pioneer treasures from the Fort's archives, including portraits, handmade samplers and toys, and wedding gowns.

Every week during the school year, whole classes of schoolchildren come to Sutter's Fort to participate in the Fort's Environmental Living Program. They arrive clad in 1840s period dress to experience what life was like in that decade, from learning how to make rope to preparing simple meals.

Sutter's Fort State Historic Park is open from 10:00 a.m. to 5:00 p.m. seven days a week except on Thanksgiving, Christmas Day, and New Years Day.

BIBLIOGRAPHY

Beck, Steve, History and Educational Programs lead at Sutter's Fort. Various research papers.

Bryant, Edwin. *What I Saw in California*. Lincoln, Nebraska: University of Nebraska Press, 1985.

Busch, Briton Cooper, ed. *Alta California 1840-1842, the Journal and Observations of William Dane Phelps, Master of the Ship Alert*. Glendale, California: The Arthur H. Clark Company, 1983.

Camp, Charles L, ed. *James Clyman, American Frontiersman. The Adventures of a Trapper and Covered Wagon Emigrant as Told in His Own Reminiscences and Diaries*. San Francisco: California Historical Society, 1928.

Chandler, Dr. Robert J., James M. Spitze and Stephen Zovickian. "A Hoax Gone Awry: E Clampus Vitus and Sir Francis Drake's 1579 Plate of Brasse." The California Territorial Quarterly No. 106, 2016.

Davis, William Heath. *Seventy-five Years in California*. Washington, DC: Westphalia Press edition, 2015.

Delgado, James P. *Witness to Empire, the Life of Antonio Maria* Suñol. Sourisseau Academy for California State and Local History, San Jose State University, 1977.

Detwiler, Justice B., ed. *Who's Who in California, A Biographical Directory 1928-29*. San Francisco: Who's Who Publishing Company, 1929.

Dillinger, William C. *The Gold Discovery—James Marshall and the California Gold Rush*. California Department of Parks and Recreation, 1990.

Dunbar, Seymour, ed. *A Transcript of the Fort Sutter Papers*. Edward Eberstadt, publisher, 1921.

Erwin, Gail S. *A Finding Aid to the Harry C. Peterson Collection at the California State Museum Resource Center*. Typescript, May 2004.

Frémont, John Charles. *Memoirs of My Life*. Cooper Square Press edition, 2001.

Frémont, Brevet Col. J. C. *The Exploring Expedition to the Rocky Mountains, Oregon and California to which is added a Description of the Physical Geography of California with Recent Notices of the Gold Region*. Buffalo: Geo. H. Derby and Co., 1851.

Gilmore, N. Ray and Gladys Gilmore. *Readings in California History* Chapter 21, Journal of John Bidwell. New York: Thomas Y. Crowell Company 1966.

Gregson, James and Eliza. *The Gregson Memoirs, Containing Mrs. Eliza Gregson's "Memory" and the Statement of James Gregson*. San Francisco: Reprinted from California Historical Society Quarterly Vol. XIX No. 2, June 1940.

Gudde, Erwin G. *Sutter's Own Story, The Life of General John Augustus Sutter and the History of New Helvetia in the Sacramento Valley*. New York: G. P. Putnam's Sons, 1936.

Gudde, Erwin C. and Elisabeth K. Gudde, translators and editors. *From St. Louis to Sutter's Fort, 1846*. University of Oklahoma Press, 1961.

Holliday, J.S. *Rush for Riches, Gold Fever and the Making of California*. Oakland Museum of California and University of California Press, 1999.

Holmes, Kenneth L., ed. *Covered Wagon Women – Diaries & Letters from the Western Trails, 1850*. Lincoln: University of Nebraska Press, Bison Books Edition, 1996.

Jones, Thomas C., compiler. *Shaping the Spirit of America* (articles from Harper's and Century Magazines). "The First Emigrant Train to California," and "Life in California Before the Gold Discovery" by John Bidwell, pp. 91, 112. Chicago: J. G. Ferguson Publishing Company, 1964.

Kantor, J.R.K., ed. *Grimshaw's Narrative*. Sacramento Book Collectors Club, 1964.

Kelly, John, and George Stammerjohan. "John Sutter and His Fort." *Dogtown Territorial Quarterly* Number 19, Fall 1994.

Kibbey, Mead, ed. *Facsimile Reproduction of the California State Library Copy of J. Horace Culver's Sacramento City Directory for the Year 1851, With a History of Sacramento to 1851, Biographical Sketches, and Informative Appendices.* Sacramento: California State Library Foundation, 2000.

Kibbey, Mead, ed. *Samuel Colville's Sacramento Directory for the Year 1853-54, Together with a History of Sacramento written by Dr. John F. Morse.* Sacramento: California State Library Foundation, 1997.

Kimball, Richard S. and Barney Neal. *Native Sons of the Golden West.* Charleston, South Carolina: Arcadia Publishing Image of America Series, 2005.

Künzel, Dr. Heinrich. *Upper California, A Geographical Description for the Purpose of German Emigration and Settlement.* Darmstadt, Germany, August 1848. Translated from the German by Anthony and Max Knight. San Francisco: The Book Club of California, 1967.

Kyle, Douglas E., editor, 5th edition. *Historic Spots in California.* Stanford University Press, 2002.

Lewis, Donovan. *Pioneers of California, True Stories of Early Settlers in the Golden State.* San Francisco: Scottwell Associates, 1993.

McDonald, Lois H. "Samuel Neal of Rancho Esquon," Parts 1 and 2. *Dogtown Territorial Quarterly*, issues #6 and #7, 1991.

Miller, Robert Ryal. *Juan Alvarado, Governor of California 1836-1842.* University of Oklahoma Press, 1998.

Morgan, Dale, editor. *Overland in 1846: Diaries and Letters of the California-Oregon Trail* Vol. I. University of Nebraska Press, 1993.

Phelps, William Dane. *Fore and Aft; or, Leaves From The Life of an Old Sailor.* Boston: Nichols & Hall, 1871.

Rensch, Hero Eugene. "Sutter's Fort 1848-1850: Size, Location and Direction of Walls – A Report on Research." Typescript prepared for Sutter's Fort State Historical Monument, June 1955.

Rensch, H. Eugene. "The True Bearing of Sutter's Fort." Prepared for Division of Beaches and Parks, printed in News and Views Supplement newsletter, July 1960.

Rogers, Fred Blackburn, ed. *A Navy Surgeon in California 1846-1847, the Journal of Marius Duvall.* San Francisco: John Howell, 1957.

Smith, Dottie. "Pierson B. Reading." Shasta County Biographies, online.

Steger, Gertrude A. "A Chronology of the Life of Pierson Barton Reading." *California Historical Society Quarterly* Vol. 22, December 1943.

Stewart, George R. *Ordeal by Hunger, the Story of the Donner Party.* Houghton Mifflin Company, 1960 edition.

Sutter, et al. *New Helvetia Diary, A Record of Events Kept by John A. Sutter and His Clerks.* San Francisco: Grabhorn Press, in arrangement with The Society of California Pioneers, 1939.

Sutter's Fort archival collections, provided by Curator Nancy Jenner.

A Tribute to Captain John A. Sutter, program booklet for the General John A. Sutter statue dedication. Sacramento, California: Printed by Corporate Press, October 1987.

Wiggins, William. "Reminiscences of William Wiggins who came to California in 1840." Manuscript dictated to Thomas Savage for the Bancroft Library, 1877.

Wilber, Marguerite Eyer, editor and translator. *A Pioneer at Sutter's Fort, 1846-1850; the Adventures of Heinrich Lienhard.* Los Angeles: The Califa Society, 1941.

Wilkes, Charles, U.S.N. Commander. *Narrative of the United States Exploring Expedition During the Years 1838, 1938, 1840, 1841, 1842.* Philadelphia: Lea & Blanchard, 1845.

Newspapers

Alta California (San Francisco)
Californian (San Francisco)
Sacramento Bee
Sacramento Daily Union
San Francisco Call
Tribune, Enterprise and Scimitar (Healdsburg)

PIONEERS AND EVENTS
IN THE NARRATIVE

Nicolaus Allgeier
James "Old Wheat" Atkinson
Billy Baldridge
John Bartleson
Alden Bayley
Bear Flag Revolt
John Bidwell
Josiah Belden
Jarvis & Truman Bonney
Patrick & Peggy Breen
Thomas Westly Bradley
Samuel Brannan
California Gold Rush
Dr. Benjamin Carman
John Chamberlain
Joseph Ballinger Chiles
James C. Coates
Nathan Coombs
Charles Covillaud
James Clyman
Octave Custot
John Daubenbiss
Nicholas "Cheyenne" Dawson
Dr. W. Grove Deal
Elitha Donner
Donner Party rescue
William Eddy
William Elliot
Mary Eyre
Ephraim Fairchild
Charles Flügge

Captain Joseph Folsom
William M. Foster
Dr. Victor Fourgeaud
John Charles Frémont
John Gantt
Paul Geddes aka Talbot Green
Dr. William Gildea
Archibald Gillespie
William Gordon
Isaac Graham
Mary Ann Graves
James & Eliza Gregson
John Grigsby
Pablo Guitiérrez
Lansford Hastings
Samuel J. Hensley
Nancy Hess
Rufus Hitchcock
William & Susan Ide
James "Jimmy" John
William Johnson
Andrew Kelsey
Nancy & Benjamin Kelsey
Sebastian Keyser
William Henry Knight
Samuel & Rebecca Kyburz
Thomas O. Larkin
Peter Lassen
Jacob Leese
Sebastian Keyser
William Leidesdorff

Heinrich Lienhard
William N. Loker
Michael McClellan
Perry McCoon
William McCutchen
Milton McGee
George McKinstry, Jr.
Green McMahon
John Marsh
Henry Marshall
James Wilson Marshall
Dr. James S. Martin
Colonel Richard B. Mason
Mexican-American War
Micheltorena Campaign
John and Daniel Murphy
Mary Murphy (Covillaud)
Martin Murphy, Sr.
Martin Murphy, Jr.
Samuel Neal
Samuel Norris
Michael Nye
William Northgrave
Lt. Edward O.C. Ord
J.D. Perkey
Captain William Dane Phelps
Charles E. Pickett
Harriet Murphy Pike
Priest, Lee & Company
Pierson B. Reading
James and Margret Reed
Allen Sanders
Lewis C. Sagat
Moses Schallenberger
Robert Sempl

Thomas Shadden
Lt. William T. Sherman
John Sinclair
Peter Slater
Charles C. Smith
Jacob Snyder
Charles Southard
Elisha Crosby Stephens
Charles Stone
August Sutter
John A. Sutter
William Swasey
Granville Swift
Dr. F. Walton Todd
William Todd
Richard D. & Olive Torney
    (Lawson)
Francis (Yount) &
    Bartlett Vines
Jean Jacque Vioget
James, John, Squire &
    Isaac Williams
William Winter
John Wooden
Joseph Wadleigh
Joel & Mary Walker
Captain William Warner
Charles Weber
William Wiggins
Peter & Jenny Wimmer
Elizabeth Yount
George Yount
George & Dorothea
    Wolfinger Zins

ABOUT THE AUTHOR

Cheryl Anne Stapp has served as a volunteer docent at Sutter's Fort State Historic Park for several years. She lives with her husband in Sacramento, in bygone days an important Gold Rush town and stagecoach center.

Visit her website "California's Olden Golden Days" at https://CherylAnneStapp.com

OTHER BOOKS BY CHERYL ANNE STAPP:
Available from Amazon.com and other selected retailers

Before The Gold Rush—
The Sinclairs of Rancho Del Paso, 1840-1849

The Stagecoach in Northern California:
Rough Rides, Gold Camps & Daring Drivers

Sacramento Chronicles—A Golden Past

Disaster & Triumph:
Sacramento Women, Gold Rush Through the Civil War

Made in the USA
Middletown, DE
11 May 2019